Maltby Ma

The Develo
Mining Community

Dave Fordham

Published by Fedj-el-Adoum Publishing
3 Adelaide Road, Norton, Doncaster, South Yorkshire, DN6 9EW

© Fedj-el-Adoum Publishing & Dave Fordham 2015

ISBN 978-09562864-5-1

First Edition 2015

Acknowledgements

The author would like to thank the following for their assistance in compiling this work: Thomas Best, Brian Brownsword, Brian Elliott, Richard Fordham, John Fordham, Paul Fox, Andrew McGarrigle, Jeremy Neal, David Packer, John Petch, Alice Rodgers, John Ryan, Joan Ulley, Helen Wallder, Tim Wolverson and the staff of Derbyshire Archives, Doncaster Archives, Rotherham Archives and Sheffield Archives. Acknowledgment is also extended to Doncaster Local Studies Library for allowing access to contemporary newspaper records from *The Doncaster Gazette* and *The Doncaster Chronicle;* and the staff of The University of Birmingham Library for viewing their holdings of *The Colliery Guardian.* I would like to especially thank Alice Rodgers and the Maltby Local History Society for suggesting improvements to the manuscript and Thomas Best for allowing the publication of his family records and photographs. Finally I would like to thank the many picture postcard publishers whose work has been used to illustrate this publication, in particular Edgar Leonard Scrivens and James Simonton & Sons. Unless otherwise attributed, all illustrations featured in this publication are from the author's collection and all attempts to attribute copyright have been made.

Cover Illustration

This superbly detailed scene at Maltby Colliery has been captured in a postcard published in 1910 by Regina Press Photographers, one of a series of postcard views commissioned by the colliery company to celebrate the striking of coal at the No.2 shaft. The view is dominated by the wooden temporary headgear above No.1 shaft (left) which was used to sink the shaft, the winding apparatus powered by the temporary steam winding engine housed in the shed (centre). On the right, the wooden headgear at No.2 shaft has recently been dismantled and the permanent steel headgear and brick heapstead (see Glossary) structure erected in its place. In the foreground two carts are being loaded with coal from the row of Dinnington Colliery private owner wagons, possibly for use on the site or for land sales to Maltby Village. Maltby Colliery was not yet producing its own coal and was reliant upon imported coal brought in via the South Yorkshire Joint Railway from nearby Dinnington Colliery. (John Petch Collection)

Maltby Main Colliery

The Development of a Mining Community

Frontispiece: This delightful pen and ink study of Maltby Colliery's No.2 shaft by an unknown artist was one of a number of similar illustrations that were published in the book Yorkshire Amalgamated Collieries: Modern Methods of Coal Production and Shipment (c1928) a publication issued to celebrate the successful amalgamation of Denaby, Cadeby, Dinnington, Maltby and Rossington Collieries and to promote the formation of Yorkshire Amalagamated Collieries. Above the red Maltby private owner wagon are two iron buckets that form part of the pit's aerial ropeway.

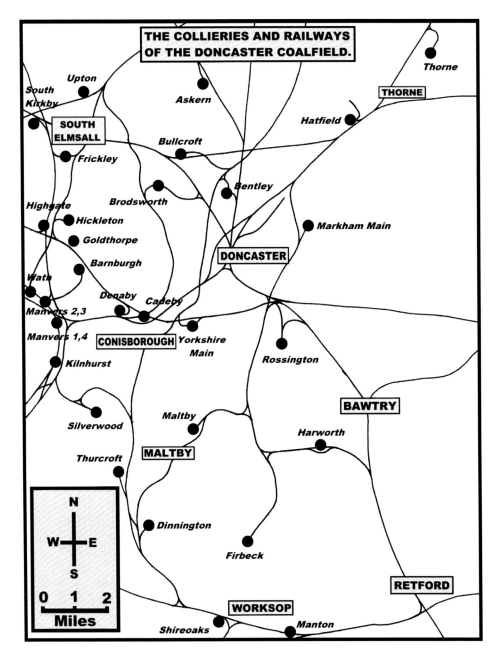

Map of the Doncaster area showing the locations of the various collieries with the railway network at its greatest extent, c1930. Maltby Main Colliery was located approximately 8 miles to the south-west of Doncaster and 6 miles east of Rotherham.

Maltby Main Colliery

The Cistercian monks certainly had an eye for selecting a picturesque location when establishing their religious houses in the 12th Century, as evidenced by the location of their monasteries at Fountains, Rievaulx and Byland in North Yorkshire. This trend continued with the foundation of Roche Abbey in 1147, located in an isolated rocky ravine at the confluence of two streams. Some of the actual abbey buildings were built over the larger of these streams, known as the Maltby Dike, as approximately a mile upstream, the stream flowed to the south of the small agricultural village of Maltby, itself mentioned in the Doomsday Book.

Unbeknown to the monks of Roche Abbey and the villagers of Maltby at the time was the fact that at depth, concealed beneath a cover of younger limestone rocks, lay a series of rock strata totalling 1,500 yards in thickness termed the Coal Measures. Despite the name, the Coal Measures are largely compiled of a series of alternating bands of sandstones, shales and clays together with occasional coal seams, paramount amongst which was a coal seam known as the Barnsley Seam.

Following the dissolution of Roche Abbey in 1538, its site and nearby lands passed through various hands before being brought together with other land to create the nucleus of the Sandbeck estate. In 1724, this estate was willed to Thomas Lumley who, on the death of his brother in 1739, became the third Earl of Scarbrough. His son, the fourth Earl, chose to make Sandbeck his home. He commissioned James Paine to reconstruct the house and employed Lancelot 'Capability' Brown to landscape the park and incorporate the ruins of Roche Abbey as a 'romantic ruin', as was fashionable at the time.

Thus in the years leading up to the turn of the 20th Century, the area was largely dominated by the local agricultural estates with most of the residents of the nearby hamlet of Stone earning their living from working on the Sandbeck estate whilst many of the villagers of Maltby found employment on the local Maltby Hall, Hellaby Hall and Hooton Levitt Hall estates or worked as agricultural labourers on the numerous tenanted farms. Some of the cottages in Maltby were owner occupied and a small number also served as holiday homes kept by families from Rotherham and Sheffield, who would spend the summer in the pleasant rural surroundings of Maltby.

However, by 1900 change was rapidly approaching the rural idyll of the Maltby area. At the time, the global demand for coal was increasing by 4% per year and the UK was the world's leading exporter of coal. As well as the export trade, domestic consumption was increasing as the country was reliant upon coal to fuel its furnaces of industry, its railway and shipping networks and its growing domestic use by a rapidly increasing population. Industrialists were keen to exploit the nation's coal reserves and landowners, enticed with the prospect of receiving large royalty payments, were similarly keen to see their coal reserves exploited. By the close of the 19th Century, two large collieries were established to the south and west of Maltby at Silverwood and Dinnington and consequently mining engineers began to turn their eyes towards the Sandbeck estate, keen to tap the great riches of coal that lay beneath.

Sandbeck Park as depicted on a postcard by Edgar Scrivens c1908. As well as owning the Sandbeck estate, the Lumley family also owned the Lumley Castle estate in County Durham, the Glentworth estate in Lincolnshire and a coastal agricultural estate where they promoted the development of the seaside resort of Skegness. In 1904, Aldred Lumley, the 10th Earl of Scarbrough, signed a mining lease for coal beneath the estate. Today, Richard Lumley, the 13th Earl of Scarbrough, remains in residence at Sandbeck.

In 1898, Dalton Main Collieries Ltd. was formed with a capital of £200,000, to acquire the small Roundwood Colliery near Rotherham and establish a large pit at Silverwood, some 3 miles to the west of Maltby, in order to exploit the coal in the Thrybergh, Wickersley and Bramley areas beneath the estates of the Fullerton family of Thrybergh Hall, and the Bosvile family of Ravenfield Park, and the Dalton estate in the possession of the Foljambe family of Osberton Hall. Sinking commenced in April 1900 and the Barnsley seam was encountered in December 1903 at a depth of 746 yards. The colliery was an immediate success and by 1910 Silverwood Colliery could claim to be the largest pit in the Yorkshire Coalfield at the time, employing a workforce of 3,228, and generating substantial profits from an output of over 1,000,000 tons per year.

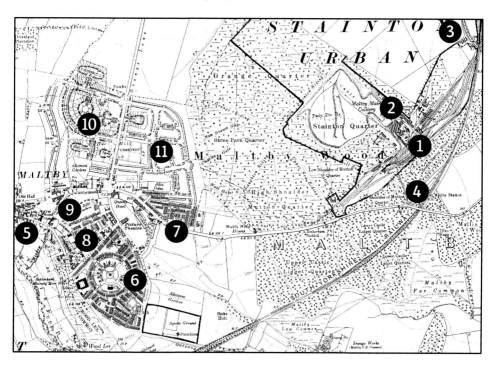

The Maltby area as shown on the Ordnance Survey 6" map of 1930 with the locations of the various features referred to in the text:
1 Maltby colliery, 2 Site of Tin Town, 3 Scotch Springs, 4 Maltby Station, 5 Maltby old village, 6 Model Village, 7 Admirals' Estate, 8 Poets' Estate, 9 Dorlonco Estate, 10 Industrial Housing Association Estate, 11 Maltby Urban District Council 'Woodlands Estate' (Crown Copyright Reserved)

Located 4 miles to the south of Maltby at Dinnington, the Sheffield Coal Company had leased a royalty of 4,000 acres belonging to the Duke of Leeds and the Althorpe family of Dinnington Hall. The Sheffield Coal Company were looking to exploit this royalty but they lacked the financial power and engineering expertise to develop a large colliery; therefore they invited the Sheepbridge Coal & Iron Company Ltd. of Chesterfield to join them as joint partners in the venture. In 1900, the Dinnington Main Coal Company Ltd. was formed with a capital of £187,500 and Sheepbridge contributed half of the capital. The first sod at Dinnington Colliery was cut in September 1902 and the shafts reached the Barnsley seam on August 23rd 1904 at a depth of 667 yards. Coal production was rapidly developed and, like neighbouring Silverwood Colliery, by 1913 the venture at Dinnington had become a success producing nearly 800,000 tons of coal that year.

The involvement of the Sheepbridge Coal and Iron Company with the Dinnington undertaking in 1900 had come at a most fortuitous time for the Chesterfield concern. In 1856, William and John Fowler had established an iron foundry, blast furnace and coke ovens near the village of Sheepbridge (hence the name of the company) and they purchased three small collieries located nearby to fuel their industrial ensemble. In 1864, the Fowler brothers' venture was restructured as The Sheepbridge Coal & Iron Company Ltd., one of 47 limited liability companies established by Henry Pochin and David Chadwick. These two men represented a group of London and Manchester investors who were looking to diversify their incomes by investing capital in new companies exploiting the expanding coal and steel industries. The issuing of shares to the public allowed the Sheepbridge Company to raise revenue to fuel its expansion plans and they subsequently developed several collieries in Derbyshire. However, by 1900, declining coal reserves at their older pits in the Chesterfield area meant that they had to look further afield in order to maintain their coal supplying contracts and uphold their profits. Thus, the company turned its attention to the concealed coalfield of South Yorkshire. The invitation to join in the development of Dinnington Colliery had proved remarkably successful and they were anxious to secure another coal royalty, but this time, one in which they could have the majority shareholding.

A borehole completed in 1893 at South Carr near Haxey had proved the existence of numerous coal seams including the prized Barnsley seam at a depth of 1,067 yards. This borehole proved the eastwards extension of the Coal Measures strata (from their outcrop in the Barnsley and Rotherham areas), into the Doncaster area, concealed beneath a cover of much younger Permian limestones and Triassic sandstones - hence the term 'concealed coalfield' as the coal bearing strata were not present at the surface. Therefore great riches lay waiting in the concealed coalfield for industrialists with financial muscle and engineering expertise. Between 1896 and 1904, total UK profits from coal mining had quadrupled thus the financial incentives for new colliery developments were certainly beneficial. However, with coal laying at such depth in the concealed coalfield, it would require the latest technological advances in mining engineering to enable the successful exploitation of these reserves. For a profit to be generated, each of the collieries of this new coalfield would have to command a huge royalty of up to 10,000 acres and employ a workforce of around 3,000 men with the aim of producing 1,000,000 tons of coal per year, all of this set in a rural background with no pre-existing railway connections and very little by the way of a local workforce. This in turn resulted in the need to construct a new settlement to house the colliery personnel, together with various shops, schools, churches etc., to service this new population. A tall order indeed and one that the Sheepbridge Coal & Iron Company believed they could meet at Maltby.

Concurrently with the move to develop large collieries by the industrialists of the day, was the urge by the landed gentry to encourage such developments as coal royalties could provide an extensive addition to estate incomes. At the time, most of the mineral rights in Maltby Parish and the adjoining Stainton Parish were controlled by the Sandbeck estate. In fact the Sandbeck Agent had been recently purchasing land in the Maltby and Tickhill areas to add to the Sandbeck acreage in order to make the enlarged royalty an even more commercially attractive prospect. In 1900, Lord Scarbrough, aware of the potential mineral wealth beneath his estate, commissioned a report by a mining surveyor into the possibilities of siting a colliery on the estate. Finally in 1902, the Sheepbridge Company approached the Sandbeck estate with a view to securing a coal lease. Negotiations were successful and in 1904 Lord Scarbrough granted Sheepbridge a lease for a period of 60 years to exploit the Barnsley seam beneath his 4,500 acre estate, over which he held the mineral rights.

At neighbouring Silverwood and Dinnington Collieries, it had been a relatively straight forward operation to construct a short railway branch line a couple of miles in length to link up the colliery sites with the pre-existing national rail network. However, at Maltby, the nearest established railway was several miles away. Nevertheless, as well as generating profits from the exploitation of the coal by industrial conglomerates carving up the royalties of the new coalfield, substantial profits could also be made by the railway companies in transporting the coal from the pithead to the market place. The speculation of colliery companies in turning their attention to exploiting the coalfield in the rural district between Doncaster and Worksop in turn generated a scramble for proposed railway lines through the district from five different railway companies; The Great Central Railway, The Great Northern Railway, The North Eastern Railway, The Midland Railway and The Lancashire & Yorkshire Railway.

To have five competing railway lines serving Maltby Colliery and the other proposed collieries of the area would ultimately prove to be a ridiculous and uneconomic proposal; therefore it was soon realised that a single railway line jointly controlled by the five railway companies, sharing the construction and profits on an equal basis, would be beneficial to all. In 1902, the South Yorkshire Joint Railway (SYJR) was established to build a railway from Dinnington Colliery (where it met the Dinnington Colliery branch line to the Great Central Railway's Sheffield-Worksop line) northwards to Long Sandall near Doncaster joining the Great Central Railway's line from Sheffield to the Humber ports, ideal outlets for coal export. Various junctions were made at Black Carr near Doncaster enabling through working onto the main London to Edinburgh railway as well as allowing connections with the line to Lincoln and East Anglia and along the Dearne Valley

Railway to Wakefield and the West Riding. This would allow traffic generated on the SYJR to reach numerous destination on the railway network. Following parliamentary approval and negotiations with the various landowners, construction of the SYJR commenced in 1905, with the line finally opening for business on 1st January 1909.

Several postcards illustrating the construction of the SYJR were published by John Crowther-Cox of Rotherham in 1907, including the example shown here depicting a steam navvy excavating the limestone cutting through Maltby Common. The view looks south towards the valley of the Maltby Dike which the railway crossed by means of a high embankment. The temporary bridge carries Blyth Road across the cutting. Near this location a settlement of tin huts was provided for the navvies working on the railway. For a time local resident Fred Kitchen worked in this cutting detailing his experiences in his autobiography 'Brother to the Ox'. (Brian Brownsword Collection).

Despite the demand for coal, there was no immediate rush to develop Maltby, as Sheepbridge's engineering staff were still working at Dinnington Colliery. This was coupled with the fact that north of Dinnington, the construction of the SYJR would require extensive time-consuming engineering work including the building of Brookhouse viaduct and the construction of several deep cuttings and high embankments, including one across the valley of Maltby Dike. Whilst awaiting the arrival of the railway and the skilled workforce to sink the shafts and develop the pit, Sheepbridge approached other landowners in the area in order to increase the acreage of the Maltby royalty.

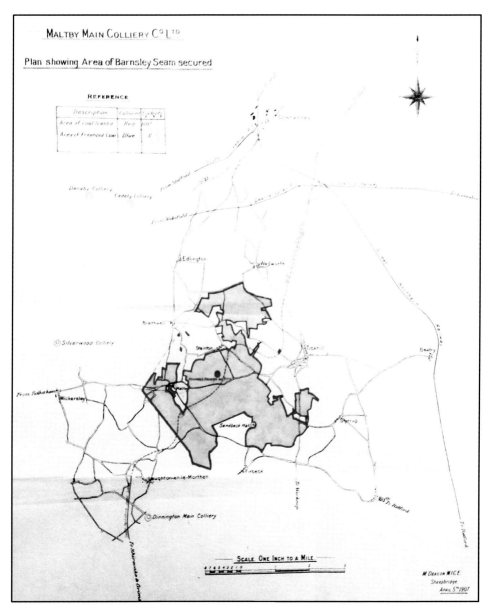

This plan, prepared by Maurice Deacon, accompanied the 1907 share prospectus for the formation of The Maltby Main Colliery Co Ltd and details the 6,031 acres of Barnsley seam leased by the end of 1906 (shaded red) together with the 31 acre freehold site to the south of Blyth Road purchased from Mr Morrell (shaded blue) with the proposed position of the pit marked in the centre of the royalty adjacent to the SYJR (dashed red line) which was currently under construction. At the time, the area of land that would ultimately form the site for Maltby Model Village had not yet been secured. Further negotiations with other landowners would eventually see the royalty total nearly 10,000 acres. (Reproduced with the consent of Rotherham Metropolitan Borough Council, Archives and Local Studies Service, Reference 942.741 MAL).

Apart from Lord Scarbrough, the other large landowners were the Reverend France-Hayhurst who owned an 800 acre estate at Wilsic Hall near Wadworth; Edward Firth who owned various lands in the Maltby area and the Schofield family of Sand Hall near Goole who owned Maltby Hall and Maltby Manor, both properties rented out to tenants. Additional smaller landowners were approached and leases secured from them, for example Mr Garnside, Mrs James, the trustees of Mr Burbeary of Stainton Hall and the Vicar of Maltby Church (for the coal beneath the glebe land in the parish). Finally an under-lease was signed with the Dalton Main Collieries Ltd. for their coal in the Braithwell area which could be more economically worked from the Maltby shafts.

Thus by the end of 1906, a royalty totalling 6,068 acres had been secured which included the purchase of the freehold of 31 acres of Maltby Meadows from local farmer Mr Morrell in July 1903 for £1,100. Negotiations were continuing for a further 2,000 acres and it was intended to eventually have a royalty of 10,000 acres from which the colliery company hoped to produce 1,000,000 tons per year for a period of 60 years or 750,000 tons per year over 80 years. They anticipated encountering the 6 foot thick Barnsley seam at a depth of between 750-850 yards. At the suggestion of Lord Scarbrough, a colliery site in the centre of the royalty was chosen in Maltby Wood within the parish of Stainton and located to the north of the road from Maltby to Tickhill, as the loss of low value woodland was financially preferable to the loss of agricultural land and the site was partially cleared of trees during the winter of 1906/7. The isolated site, nearly 2 miles from Maltby Church, was set back from the main road and located on the other side of the SYJR to Sandbeck Hall, the intention being that the railway line would act as a barrier to any intended trespass or poaching on the Sandbeck estate by the new colliery's workforce.

All the negotiations for the development of the new venture had to this point been through the management team of Sheepbridge itself, comprising Frederick Fowler (Chairman), William Jackson (General Manager) and Maurice Deacon (Managing Director); the expenses thus occurred had been met by Sheepbridge. However, in 1907 the Sheepbridge management decided to establish a subsidiary company to develop the colliery and invite private investors and members of the public to become shareholders in the new concern.

On the 1st February 1907, the Maltby Main Colliery Company Ltd. was registered with a capital of £350,000 to acquire from Sheepbridge, freehold coal and mining leases under the parishes of Blyth, Braithwell, Firbeck, Harworth, Laughton-en-le-Morthen, Maltby, Stainton and Tickhill, with the ultimate purpose of developing the colliery at Maltby. Of the £350,000 of capital required, £200,000 had been provided by Sheepbridge (giving them a majority control) with the remaining £150,000 being allotted to the general public. The first directors were nominated as:

Maurice Deacon, Whittington House, Chesterfield. (Chairman & Managing Director)
Frederick Fowler, St James Street, Sheffield.
William McConnel, Heath End House, Basingstoke.
Sir Charles McLaren, Belgrave Square, London.
Walter McLaren, Ashley Gardens, London.
William Jackson, Ringwood, Chesterfield.
Thomas Haslam, Sheepbridge Works, Chesterfield. (Secretary)

Of the above, all served as directors of Sheepbridge. Incidentally, Sir Charles McLaren (Lord Aberconway from 1911) was the grandson of Henry Pochin, who had established Sheepbridge in 1864. The new company immediately issued a share prospectus inviting members of the public to subscribe for the remainder of the £150,000 capital. The share prospectus also included a map of the Maltby area detailing the 6,037 acres of coal royalty secured, the 31 acre freehold site in Maltby that had been purchased from Mr Morrell in 1903 and the proposed position of the colliery.

The first act of the new Maltby Main Colliery Company Ltd. was to purchase the leases and the 31 acre freehold site from the Sheepbridge Company for £18,804. The reason for establishing the subsidiary company was made clear at the 1906 Sheepbridge AGM where Maurice Deacon stated that they were aiming to increase the earning power of Sheepbridge without increasing the capital of the company and that by investing in subsidiary companies, they could control a large area of coal to sell without putting all their money into one pit. From a business point of view, this method ensured they had overall control of Maltby colliery (via their 57% shareholding) but shared the cost of development with the private shareholders, whose reward would hopefully be the annual payment of a dividend on their shares.

However, it was not the intention to immediately commence sinking the shafts as first it was proposed that a short borehole would be drilled to ascertain the approximate depth of the Barnsley seam and the thickness of the overlying limestone. It wasn't deemed necessary to bore all the way to the coal seam, just to the rocks that form the upper part of the Coal Measures. From this, an estimate could be made of the expected depth and whether or not the overlying limestone and upper coal measures would prove troublesome with the potential danger of flooding and leakage from water, something that had plagued the sinking of many South Yorkshire collieries. Consequently this work, costing £2,000, was undertaken by The Vivian Boring & Exploration Company, who had drilled the boreholes to prove the viability of Bentley and Brodsworth Collieries.

To facilitate the building of the SYJR in 1906, the contractor had laid a temporary railway along the proposed route to aid construction and the moving of materials. Following the completion of a temporary branch line to the colliery site in June 1907 a start was made on transporting the plant and materials to the site via the temporary railway. Equipment used in the sinking of nearby Dinnington Colliery was moved to the new site together with several 'tin huts' (usually wooden buildings with roofs of corrugated iron) which would be used to house the 'sinkers', the name given to the specialised itinerant engineers who travelled the country and undertook the sinking of colliery shafts. The sinkers were a dedicated team of hard working (and supposedly hard drinking!) men who undertook this relatively well paid but dangerous work.

Initially entrance to the colliery site had been from Scotch Spring Lane near Stainton. In 1907, trees were felled to improve access from the Maltby-Tickhill Road. Although the SYJR contractor's line provided access for most of the materials, including coal and bricks from Dinnington Colliery for use at the surface, traction engines hauled goods via this new access road including the two steam powered winding engines that would be used for sinking the shafts. The shafts, each 20 feet in diameter, would be sunk beneath temporary wooden headgear powered by the temporary steam engines, around which the much larger permanent headgear and winding engines would be installed, ready to come into operation once coal had been reached. It was estimated that it would take two years to sink the shafts to the Barnsley Seam. The shafts were known as the No. 1 (downcast) shaft and the No. 2 (upcast) shaft and they were both estimated to strike coal at a depth of 800 yards. The names downcast and upcast were derived from the fact that fresh air would be driven down the downcast shaft to ventilate the underground workings before being expelled via the upcast shaft.

On September 3rd 1907, in the presence of Lord and Lady Scarbrough, a small ceremony was held to mark the cutting of the first sod of the No. 2 shaft of Maltby Main Colliery. On March 30th 1908 the first sod of No. 1 shaft was cut and the difficult and dangerous work of sinking the shafts commenced. A team of 150 sinkers and their families, under the direction of Mr Sykes, the master sinker, were employed to undertake the hazardous and difficult work of sinking the Maltby shafts. Mr Sykes and his team had been responsible for sinking the shafts at Dinnington Colliery and would later move on to sink the shafts at Rossington

Colliery. The sinkers and their families were housed in a temporary settlement in the Maltby colliery pit yard, which came to be informally known as 'tin town.' This consisted of a series of three rows of corrugated metal huts arranged in blocks of 6 and positioned in an area to the northwest of the shafts. The accommodation in each hut consisted of two bedrooms and a sitting room. Other huts housed workshops and offices and bunkhouses for single men as well as a communal canteen. Additionally, a tin school known as the pit school was provided by the West Riding Education Authority with a staff of 4 teachers to look after the children of the sinkers. The only shop in tin-town was a branch of the Doncaster Co-operative Society who opened the grandly named 'Stainton Co-operative Hut' which only sold basic provisions and reportedly did a roaring trade in beer and woodbines!

The tin school in the pit yard with the children of the pit sinkers gathered for the camera in 1910. The man on the left is possibly Mr. Spencer, the headmaster who was later joined by three additional teaching staff; Miss Weldon, Mr. Rickwood & Miss Horscroft. The building saw further use as a school at Rossington for the children of the sinkers at that colliery. (Photographer unknown – reproduced from the Maltby 2014 calendar with the consent of calendar sponsor Jeremy Neal Funeral Directors).

To prevent poaching and trespassing on the surrounding farmland and woodland, the tin town was partially surrounded by a large corrugated iron fence. However, despite this, trespassing and the petty thieving of potatoes and turnips from the adjacent fields caused an exchange of letters between Mr Nicholson the tenant of Stainton Manor Farm and the Sandbeck agent Sidney Ambler. Living at such a distance from a legitimate source of fresh food it is easy to see how tempting it would be for the sinkers to poach game from the adjacent Sandbeck estate together with the pilfering of food from the fields. However, no doubt it came as a relief to the local farmers when the sinkers completed their work and transferred to sink the shafts at Rossington Colliery, taking their tin town and tin school with them.

The actual process of shaft sinking was undertaken by the use of large metal buckets called hoppits and these were lowered and raised up the shafts by chains suspended from the wooden headgear above. Excavated material, blown out by dynamite and hewn by pick and shovel was loaded into the hoppits and raised to the surface. These buckets were also the means of transport to get the sinkers to the bottom of the shafts, with up to 9 men being transported within the hoppit. The work of shaft sinking was strenuous and extremely dangerous. The sinkers protected themselves from the constant incursions of water pouring into the shafts by wearing oilskins and sou'westers, and were described in contemporary newspaper reports as resembling lifeboat men and wearing boots 'that would make a Policeman blush!' During the shaft sinking process through the limestone and the sandstones of the upper coal measures, the expected water incursions were met. Initially this was pumped out and discharged via pipes into the small dyke near the Tickhill Road, causing complaints from the tenant of Sandbeck lodge Farm. However, the initial borehole that had been sunk in 1906 was converted into a water pump to supply water for use in the pit yard, which was eventually used in the steam engines and boilers and two large wooden cooling towers, as well as being piped for domestic use in the colliery village.

The demanding nature of the shaft sinking did not proceed without incident and on 31st March 1909, three of the sinkers - Sam Saunders, Charles Simons & Arthur Orton - fell to their deaths from the hoppit to the base of No.2 shaft which at that time had reached a depth of 380 yards. The subsequent inquest detailed the fact that the hoppit struck the side of the shaft 70 yards from the surface where a water pump had been installed, upending the hoppit which was believed to be unbalanced by the unfortunate occupants.

On 19th August 1909 another terrible accident occurred in No.2 shaft with the tragic death of sinker George Goodgroves. (The name is sometimes reported as Goodgrove although his great granddaughter informed me that the family name had a silent 's' at the end; hence the confusion). The pit sinker was struck by falling material which was being winched up the shaft by a chain attached to a railway locomotive. His death actually caused the raising of questions in the House of Commons as to the safety aspect of using locomotives in raising men or materials from a mine shaft. George had lived with his wife and 12 children in one of the tin huts in the pit yard and there was great concern as to the wellbeing of the family as it was well known that a colliery company could evict a widow and her children so that their accommodation could be used by another employee and his family. However, the family were still living in tin-town during the time of the 1911 census and many of the children subsequently gained work at the colliery. Following his death, a collection from the other sinkers raised £20 and this was followed by a charity cricket match between a team of sinkers and one of local workmen who were constructing the colliery housing. Lord Scarbrough purchased several tickets. The tragic deaths of the four sinkers marked the first four of 163 deaths during the working life of Maltby Colliery.

During shaft sinking operations, boundary line agreements were drawn up with neighbouring collieries in order to eliminate the possibility of an adjacent mine encroaching onto another's royalty and to facilitate the more economical working of coal reserves within the boundary areas. To the west lay Silverwood Colliery which was undergoing rapid expansion, and the proposed Thurcroft coalfield belonging to Rothervale Collieries. To the north was Edlington Colliery where shafts were currently being sunk. To the east, the owners of Silverwood Colliery were putting together another coalfield centred on Rossington whilst a private speculator was assembling leases to form the Harworth Coalfield. To the south, the Maltby royalty adjoined Dinnington Colliery, itself developing and expanding rapidly and this colliery was also interested in developing a second coalfield adjacent to Maltby at Firbeck. Following these negotiations the Maltby royalty would contain approximately 10,000 acres, from which it was hoped to sustain the colliery for a life of 100 years.

Concurrently with the process of shaft sinking, some of the permanent surface buildings were constructed, including a winding engine house for No. 2 shaft which bears a 1908 date stone as does the nearby powerhouse. An 80 foot high steel lattice headgear was erected around and above the wooden headgear of No.2 shaft, as it was intended that the permanent structure could be in place once coal had been reached. Adjacent to the power houses, a powerful steam powered fan was provided to ventilate the underground workings together with coal screening buildings which straddled the railway sidings, a 'Baum' coal washing plant to clean the coal installed by the firm of Simon Carves, 120 coke ovens, a by-product plant and finally a large chimney to service the coal fired Lancashire boilers. In 1909 the colliery company commenced the building of the permanent colliery village on a site near the old village of Maltby as it was intended to have the houses built and occupied so that a workforce was in place to immediately develop the coal faces once the shafts had intercepted the Barnsley seam.

Sinking operations underway at No.1 shaft during 1910. The wooden headgear was used to wind the hoppits up the shaft tipping their contents down a chute to the lower left of the structure into waiting wagons. The winding rope leads from the wheel to the wooden engine house on the right that housed the temporary winding engines. The Coal Mines Act (1911) decreed that any newly opened collieries employing more than 30 persons had to have headgears made from non-flammable material. Although the wooden headgears predate this act, it was never the intention at Maltby to retain them due to the fact that the strain of winding coal from great depths would have been too much for such structures. The permanent headgears and winding engine houses would later be orientated away from the photographer. Behind the headgear can be seen one of the colliery's two wooden cooling towers. These towers, with a capacity of 150,000 gallons per hour, condensed the steam from the Lancashire boilers and returned the warm water back to them, thereby greatly increasing their efficiency. Visible in the distance on the lower left are the rows of sinkers huts comprising the settlement of 'tin town'. (Postcard by Regina Press Photographers, John Ryan Collection).

Additional buildings in the pit yard included a suite of colliery offices and a rather grand semi-detached villa to provide accommodation for the colliery agent and the head engineer. Plans for a rather elaborately designed canteen featuring a domed structure were lodged by Maurice Deacon with Doncaster Rural District Council in 1908 but this unusual building appears not to have been built and canteen facilities were provided in wooden huts. A terrace of 6 'mechanics' houses' was built adjacent to Scotch Spring Lane. These were provided to house 'on call' colliery officials including the ambulance room attendant, colliery engineer, blacksmith and the horse ostler (the man responsible for the care of the colliery's pit ponies). This development subsequently became known as the hamlet of Scotch Springs. Adjacent to Tickhill Road, two large villas for the colliery manager and under-manger were constructed in 1911. The first Maltby Colliery manager was Mr Dyson, who came from Dinnington in 1908 with Mr

Roberts formerly of Shirebrook Colliery appointed as his under manager whilst Basil Pickering was appointed colliery agent. In 1912, Mr Dyson moved to manage Rossington Colliery and he was replaced with Mr Soar, his former replacement at Dinnington Colliery.

On June 18th 1910, the No. 2 shaft finally encountered the Barnsley seam at a depth of 820 yards. The coal was 8ft 4" thick which pleased the management and they hoped to extract the lower 5 feet of this leaving the poorer quality upper part to form a roof. Maurice Deacon sent a telegram to Lord Scarbrough confirming the find but, perhaps in his excitement, stated incorrectly that the depth was 898 yards.

To celebrate the discovery of coal, the colliery company entertained their workforce and the local population, a total of 400-500 people, to a celebratory feast hosted in a large marquee on a field adjacent to Maltby Hall. A commemorative lamp containing the first piece of coal brought to the surface was presented to Lord Scarbrough on July 9th 1910. At the time the No. 1 shaft had attained a depth of 460 yards and it finally struck the Barnsley seam in January 21st 1911. To celebrate, Lord Scarbrough sent a donation to be divided among the 310 employees at the colliery which included the team of 102 sinkers

During 1911, a second 80 foot high steel lattice headgear was erected over No.1 shaft. Each of the new headgears was linked to a large brick built winding engine house which contained a Markham & Company horizontal twin cylinder steam engine installed in 1910 together with a series of Lancashire condensing boilers. The No. 2 engine house had been completed in 1908 and with the completing of the No.1 engine house in 1911, this allowed the dismantling of the wooden headgears and removal of the temporary winding engines now that the permanent apparatus was in place. Beneath the headgears a heapstead building connected the shafts with the screens. The heapstead building beneath the upcast shaft extended upwards to nearly enclose the steel headgear above with a brick tower. This had the effect of increasing the draught which aided the underground ventilation. With practically all the surface buildings in place, the coal located and the first phase of a mining village completed, the colliery was ready to commence coal production. However, before commercial production could start, work to open out the pit bottom and develop the various coal faces would have to be undertaken.

On July 7th 1911, Maurice Deacon, speaking at the annual general meeting of the Maltby Main Colliery Company, delivered a progress update to shareholders. In developing the pit, the company had so far spent £237,859 of the £350,000 capital and they were presently raising 1,000 tons a week, mostly from the opening out of various roadways and tunnels through what was known as the shaft pillar, a circular area of coal 900 yards in diameter surrounding the base of the shafts and left in place in order to protect the surface buildings from the effects of subsidence. The winding plant had been laid out for an output of 6,000 tons per day although if this was required they would have to enlarge the screens and sidings which currently had a capacity to handle up to 3,000 tons per day. 200 full time miners were now employed and 144 houses in the first phase of Maltby Model Village had been completed with a further 122 currently under construction.

In 1911, the 200 men employed at the colliery produced an annual output of 68,675 tons, mostly derived from tunnelling through the coal seam in order to open up the coal faces. However, during this work an explosion killed 3 of the workers. The Barnsley seam is notoriously gassy and gives off highly flammable methane emissions. Working of this gassy seam would require adequate and sufficient ventilation, something that would come to light when a second explosion would strike the colliery on its darkest day in 1923.

The wooden headgear and winding engine house depicted in the previous illustration were replaced with the steel lattice headgear and brick built winding engine house depicted in this Edgar Scrivens postcard of 1914, the gable end of the No.1 engine house containing a prominent cast iron 1911 date stone. Following the reconstruction programme in the 1960s, the winding engine houses were demolished and the 1908 date stone from the No.2 engine house was later positioned together with one of the winding wheels at the entrance to the colliery on Tickhill Road. The steel No.1 headgear survived the reconstruction schemes and lasted until the closure of the pit in 2013.

A superbly detailed c1912 Regina Press Postcard of No. 2 upcast shaft with its steel lattice headgear partially encased in a brick collar extension from the heapstead structure beneath. Coal filled tubs were wound to a level about 30 feet above the ground surface before they passed along the gantry on the right to the screens building where they discharged their loads into the tipplers and grading machinery contained within the screens. Empty tubs were then hauled up the incline for return to the underground workings. (John Ryan Collection)

Despite the explosion in the previous year, work continued to develop the underground workings throughout 1912 with the successful opening up of the various coal faces contained within the 8 districts of the mine. The coal faces were worked by the advancing longwall method in a direction away from the shafts. Following the extraction of the coal the pit props supporting the roof were moved forward as the face advanced. The worked out void left behind, known as the gob, was allowed to naturally collapse. The coal was mined by pick and shovel and hand loaded into tubs which were then pulled by an endless rope haulage system or by one of the Colliery's pit ponies to the No.1 shaft bottom. This shaft was equipped with a cage containing 3 decks each holding 4 tubs; thus 12 tubs could be wound up the shaft during each winding. Following its emergence at the surface the coal was tipped into screens where it was sorted and graded into different classes and unwanted stone removed. Following washing, the coal was dispatched from screens into a fleet of private owner wagons ready to be taken for sale. The railway companies did not provide wagons to transport the coal; therefore Maltby Colliery purchased around 1,000 7-plank private owner wagons, all painted red and emblazoned with the lettering MALTBY MAIN in white shaded with black highlighting. Above this was written the tag line BEST SOUTH YORKSHIRE BARNSLEY COAL. The rakes of wagons departed the sidings at frequent intervals northwards via the SYJR with its connections into the national rail network near Doncaster.

Approximately half the production was intended for export to foreign markets, chiefly via the Humber ports of Goole, Grimsby and Immingham. The remainder was destined for British markets, particularly steelworks and gasworks, although the best quality coal found favour with many of London's household fire places where the appropriately named 'Barnsley Brights' were burned.

To undertake the work of coal production, the colliery recruited 1,000 men from all over the country, particularly form the older coalfields of Staffordshire, Warwickshire, Northumberland and Derbyshire together with men from Ireland. Those early days must have contained a considerable mix of accents! The workforce was supplemented by local men, many of whom had previously worked on the agricultural estates of the area and who were attracted to the colliery with its promise of higher wages and ready accommodation. One person who fell into this latter group was Fred Kitchen who originally worked on the farms of the Sandbeck estate before moving to the model village to take work at the colliery. Fred subsequently described his experiences of working on the land, working as a navvy during the construction of the SYJR and as a colliery surface worker, in his autobiography *Brother to the Ox*.

Despite this rapid increase in progress and the fact that all of the £350,000 share capital had now been subscribed, chairman Maurice Deacon was clearly unsatisfied when he presented the 1912 annual general meeting. His 1,000 men had produced 294,184 tons of coal that year but Mr Deacon wanted to employ 4,000 men in order for the colliery to produce over 1,000,000 tons of coal per year. Mr. Deacon stated that "the company was doing the best they could do by building a model village containing cottages of an improved type which were well built and convenient with small front gardens and backyards. 400 houses had been completed in the model village and they had proposals to build a second development to the north of Tickhill Road adjacent to the Managers and Under-managers houses". One of the problems with recruiting sufficient men was competition with adjoining collieries as Silverwood, Dinnington, and Edlington were also rapidly expanding at the same time and further collieries were planned to the east of Maltby at Rossington, Harworth and Firbeck. Each of these pits was looking to employ several thousand men.

Upper: *Construction underway in 1911 with the steel headgear of No. 1 shaft nearing completion but lacking its winding wheels, together with the steel frame work of the screen buildings under course of erection.*
Lower: *The photographer returned to record the completion of Maltby Colliery in 1914 capturing a busy scene as rakes of the colliery company's private owner wagons await loading beneath the screens building. (Both Postcards by Edgar Scrivens).*

Despite the problem with recruiting a sufficient workforce at Maltby, progress continued to be made during 1913 with the colliery recording its first profit of £6,324 (although no dividend was paid, the profit being carried forward to the following year's accounts) with coal production reaching 415,000 tons that year. Progress continued throughout 1914 when the colliery recorded a profit of £3,378. Again no dividend was paid and the profit was carried forward to the following year.

By the outbreak of the First World War, negotiations with minor landholders and the further direct purchase of land had increased the royalty to 9,500 acres. A total of 552 houses had been completed in the model village with a further 181 houses in the Tickhill Road area; a total of 733 houses and it was planned to build another estate to the east of Morrell Street. However, the expected dramatic increase in coal production had been retarded by a lack of men with the 1,500 currently employed only able to mine 500,000 tons of coal. By 1915, the Rotherham Advertiser reported that 350 Maltby miners had enlisted as soldiers, and this figure had increased to 460 by the following year when the colliery company delivered its annual report to shareholders, despite the fact that mining was a protected occupation. Interestingly, the Maltby Main Colliery Roll of Honour, which for a long time hung in the Church of the Ascension in the model village, only listed 316 names of men from the colliery who served in World War I.

The remainder of the war years were marked by a steady recovery. Despite the initial drop in manpower, recruitment continued apace and the war effort had the dramatic effect of increasing the demand for and price of coal. Consequently the colliery made substantial profits during 1916 and 1917 declaring its first dividends of 5% and 10% respectively, no doubt to the relief of the shareholders who had so far not seen any return on their investment. Continued development at the colliery had been met by a loan of £250,000 from Sheepbridge. Thus in 1918 it was decided to increase Maltby Main's share capital from £350,000 to £700,000 and Sheepbridge reduced the loan to £50,000 in lieu of the parent company taking up a further 200,000 shares in Maltby Colliery, giving them a total of 400,000 with the remaining 300,000 shares being taken by members of the public. Maurice Deacon stated that the increased capital would enable the company to repay loans which had been secured to meet expenditure on the pit, wagons, coke ovens, by-product plant, housing and land. The colliery had cost more than expected due to the greater depth of coal than originally thought and the higher rates of wages and cost of materials. Seen through 21st Century eyes, it now seems incredible that £700,000 was sufficient to sink and equip Maltby Main Colliery and build 733 houses, such is the rate of inflation!

Between 1917 and 1921, although still functioning as a private company, Maltby Colliery and the rest of the UK coalfield had been compulsorily placed under government control as part of the war effort and increased production during this time had assisted Maltby Main in recording its first profits. However on reversion to private control in April 1921, the country's colliery owners immediately implemented a wage reduction as they refused to match the salaries the miners had received during the period of government control. Consequently a national 3 month long strike was called which locally had the effect of reducing production to 334,000 tons that year. When other trade unions failed to support the national strike, the miners were left with no option but to accept the reduced terms offered by the management, who in turn blamed this on the increased cost of materials due to the rapidly increasing rate of inflation at the time. Therefore the Maltby miners reluctantly returned to work under the new conditions.

In 1912 a coking plant was installed at Maltby Colliery to the northeast of the pit by the Manchester engineering concern, Simon-Carves Ltd. This Company had been established in 1878 by two Frenchman, Henry Simon & Francois Carves, to perfect the recovery of chemical by-products from the treatment of coal, together with the production of coke. In this postcard view by Edgar Scrivens, dated 1914, conveyor structures supply the large bunker building with coal which was fired in the battery of coking ovens (lower right); the emissions exhausted via the tall brick chimney centre. Simon-Carves was also responsible for the construction of the screens and coal washing plant together with the later installation of the aerial ropeway. Behind the coke ovens lay the original access to the pit site from Scotch Spring Lane in Stainton.

Maltby Colliery viewed from the area formerly occupied by Tin-Town. In prominent view are the two wooden cooling towers and the large chimney that serviced the power house and winding engines. The second chimney on the left belongs to the colliery's coking and by-product recovery plant (Postcard c1913 by James Simonton, Andrew McGarrigle Collection)

In 1922, Maurice Deacon resigned his position as Chairman due to ill health. Maurice Deacon had entered the mining industry in 1867 and became a fully competent mining and civil engineer and he was instrumental in the development of Dinnington, Maltby and Rossington Collieries. He was also a self-taught architect and helped to design the early colliery housing and the estate layouts at these pits. His place as Maltby Chairman was taken by Charles McLaren who had since become Lord Aberconway in 1911. In 1922, coal production had returned to pre-strike levels with 560,000 tons produced that year. However, due to the uncertain economic situation at the time, Lord Aberconway declared that the colliery could only generate a profit when it produced above 750,000 tons per year. During 1921 and 1922 the colliery had made of loss of £81,862 due to the 1921 strike and the fact that the pit was producing well beneath its capacity. Once again the lack of men and accommodation for the men and their families was a contributing factor. Consequently in 1922, Maltby Main Colliery undertook a further house building programme.

An interesting development in early 1923 was the linking up of Maltby, Dinnington and Rossington collieries by an overhead electric cable. Surplus electricity generated at either of the three pits could be used by any of the others, but more importantly was the fact that electricity could be provided for the houses of the model village. During 1923 the colliery was on course to produce 800,000 tons when a terrible disaster occurred on July 28th, killing 27 men. In the months prior to this date, many small smouldering fires had been burning in the gob waste, the abandoned areas where the coal had been previously extracted. On Saturday 28th July at 9.15am, a team of 130 miners was working at extinguishing the fires by blocking off certain areas in the eastern district beneath the village of Stainton and about a mile from the pit bottom when an explosion occurred killing 27 instantly.

Almost immediately a rescue party with breathing apparatus and equipment was summoned consisting of men from surrounding collieries, Maltby Main officials and members of the Rotherham Mines Rescue, whilst a huge crowd of men, wives and family members congregated in the pit yard together with the St John's Ambulance ladies, doctors, ministers of religion and personnel from His Majesties Inspectorate of Mines. The rescue party, accompanied by Herbert Smith, the president of the Mineworkers Union, and Edward Dunn and Hughie Ross, the local union officials, descended the pit but their access to the affected area was hindered by rock falls caused by the explosion. Only the body of one man, the unusually named Original 'Reg' Renshaw, was recovered as the remainder had been instantly entombed during the explosion. Due to the dangerous conditions and the threat of further explosions a decision was made to seal off the affected district.

At first it was thought that the damage caused by the explosion would ultimately lead to the closure and abandoning of the colliery. It certainly had the short term effect of throwing the entire workforce of 2,689 employees out of work contributing to extreme hardship for the village as at the time unemployment benefits were negligible, although a small number of men were able to seek employment at nearby Rossington and Yorkshire Main Collieries. A relief fund was established to provide for the 22 widows and 57 fatherless children with the aim of raising £50,000 with the hope that the fund would also pay for the children to attend the proposed Maltby Grammar School. The colliery company donated £2,000 which was matched by a donation from the neighbouring Doncaster Collieries Association. £500 was donated by Yorkshire Main Chairman Charlie Markham and further donations came from the Lord Scarbrough and members of the public and by 1927 £16,772 had been raised.

The inquest into the death of Original Renshaw concluded that he had been accidentally killed by an explosion. His funeral, held symbolically with those of the 26 entombed miners, was held at the Church of the Ascension in the Model

Village, conducted by the Bishop of Sheffield before a huge crowd. The cortege then proceeded to Maltby Cemetery on Grange Lane where his body was laid to rest. Twenty four years later on 14th November 1947, another unidentified victim of the disaster was found during underground remedial work in the sealed off district. His remains were interred at Maltby Cemetery beneath a stone dedicated to the unknown miner.

The official enquiry into the Maltby Colliery disaster was held on 18th September 1923 at Sheffield City Hall and convened by HM Chief Inspector of Mines. The report, published the following year, concluded that the 27 men died from an explosion of methane caused by spontaneous combustion whilst undertaking work to stem outbreaks of gob fires. They were working in areas with high gas levels in the air, (methane can be explosive when in concentrations of between 5% and 12% in the air) but were not withdrawn by the colliery officials who were under the impression that, as they were fighting a gob fire, they had discretionary powers not to withdraw the men under Section 67 of the Coal Mines Act regarding the dangers from inflammable gas. No prosecutions were brought forward against any individual or the colliery company. Whatever, the reasons regarding safety or lack thereof, an intriguing reference was made in a report titled 'Development of Maltby Colliery 21 Feb 1946' by Yorkshire Amalgamated Collieries (who took control of Maltby Colliery in 1927). This internal report makes reference to the fact that Maltby Colliery "was developed under the control of mining engineers experienced in the Nottinghamshire & Derbyshire Top Hard Seam and it was found that this method of development was not suited to exploiting the gassy Barnsley seam of the Doncaster coalfield. Consequently, it had been necessary to develop working faces at Maltby on different lines under new management."

Whether their own internal report implicates any blame for the disaster on the original Sheepbridge management team is subject to individual interpretation. However, it must not be underestimated in how progressive Sheepbridge were in contributing to the development of the South Yorkshire Coalfield. They had successfully co-developed Dinnington Colliery in 1902 and taken the initiative in sinking Maltby Colliery shortly after. In 1911 they joined forces with the owners of Silverwood Colliery in opening out Rossington Colliery, followed by another partnership in the 1920s, this time with the Staveley Coal & Iron Company at Firbeck Colliery. Had it not been for the changing economic climate, they would have established a further pit at Finningley, to the east of Doncaster.

Returning to the aftermath of the pit disaster, following extensive remedial work, Maltby Colliery was declared safe at the end of August 1923. Despite the disaster, it was a great relief to the workforce who relied on wages from the pit for survival, when the colliery re-opened on 8th September and men were re-employed in small numbers. In total by the end of October, 1,000 men had been re-engaged in the pit's western districts.

Before the disaster, the workforce of 2,689 men had produced 2,800 tons of coal per day, 30% less than was needed for the colliery to break even. By 1924, only 1,850 men had been re-employed producing 1,700 tons of coal per day. Consequently the colliery recorded a heavy loss of £95,689 in the two years following the disaster. By 1925, progress was being made with returning the colliery to pre-disaster employment and production levels but it was realised that considerable investment would be needed to allow the colliery to develop its full potential to join the '1,000,000 tonners' of the Doncaster Coalfield. On January 27th 1926, the Sheepbridge management board met with Major Leslie, Chairman of Denaby and Cadeby Main Collieries Ltd, and voted to sell their £400,000 stake in Maltby Colliery to Denaby & Cadeby Main Collieries Ltd, who had accumulated a vast reserve of profits and who were prepared to complete the full development of Maltby Colliery.

During these negotiations, the Government was looking for voluntary amalgamations and consolidations of the various British colliery companies in order to facilitate more efficient operation. Naturally, this drew resistance in some areas but Major Leslie and Lord Aberconway saw the benefits of these proposals. As well as holding 400,000 shares in Maltby Colliery, Sheepbridge held 204,972 shares in Dinnington Colliery and 382,505 in Rossington Colliery. Major Leslie proposed plans to place the control of Denaby, Cadeby, Dinnington, Maltby and Rossington Collieries under a new company titled Yorkshire Amalgamated Collieries Ltd. (YAC) and on March 27th 1927 the formation of the new company was registered.

Each of the subsidiary colliery companies would continue to trade independently but its dividend would be paid to the parent company, YAC. Shareholders would receive shares in YAC in exchange for their share in the subsidiary companies, dividends being paid from the profits generated by the new parent company. 75% shareholder approval was required for the new arrangement. However, there was considerable resistance to this proposal from some of the private shareholders who held some of the capital of Maltby Main Colliery. At the annual general meeting held on February 3rd 1927 at the Royal Victoria Hotel in Sheffield, Lord Aberconway addressed the dissenting shareholders. He said that unless there was sufficient capital put into Maltby to develop it into full condition there was no alternative but to try and sell it to somebody, wind it up, or amalgamate it with another. Fortunately Lord Aberconway's pleas were heard and the Maltby shareholders voted to transfer their shares to the new company.

Lord Aberconway took on the role of the first chairman of YAC, with Major Leslie of Denaby and William Jackson of Sheepbridge taking the roles of joint managing directors. They were joined by Sir Henry Norman, W H McConnel, F J Dundas, K R Pelly and Colonel Stobart who had all served on the boards of the various subsidiary companies. The aims of YAC were to develop the coalfield controlled by Maltby and Rossington Collieries; to eliminate the boundaries between the coalfield of the subsidiary concerns, thus accessing 5,000,000 tons of coal; to establish joint selling arrangements and facilities for the joint purchase of materials; to increase coal output and the number of men employed following the development of Maltby and Rossington; and to pool financial resources and more economical working, treating and selling of the coal. It was proposed to borrow £500,000 to fully develop Maltby and Rossington Collieries.

This 1930s advertising postcard produced by Yorkshire Amalgamated Collieries, features a rake of private owner wagons posed in the front of the picture. The private owner coal wagons purchased by YAC for use at Maltby were simply emblazoned with the word MALTBY in large white letters on the side, replacing the earlier legend of 'Maltby Main: Best South Yorkshire Barnsley Coal' that had adorned the earlier fleet of wagons. This certainly had the effect of making the name more noticeable as the wagons passed through the railway network throughout the country! The gantry like structure straddling the screens is part of the apparatus that removes the waste material from the screens and washery to the small loading bunker positioned behind the fourth wagon. From this, the aerial ropeway (removed from this promotional picture long before the concept of touching up in Photoshop became fashionable, but visible in the coloured picture in the frontispiece) headed away to the left to the tipping site that would eventually come to cover the majority of Maltby Wood (John Ryan Collection).

Obviously this new arrangement would be beneficial to the Maltby Main Colliery Company and on 1st April 1927, management and officials from Denaby Colliery took over the organisation of the pit and Harold Harrison was awarded the role of Maltby Colliery manager with Major Leslie as the company chairman. The colliery had made a loss of £44,841 during the previous year, partly due to the effects of the 1926 General Strike and YAC drew up plans to extend the exploitation of the royalty in order to increase production and revenue. One of the first proposals was the sinking of two further collieries to access the coal reserves. A site at Fordales Farm near Micklebring and another near Tickhill were chosen as the locations for two new collieries. However, nothing was ever heard of these proposals again as, perhaps wisely, the new management chose to concentrate their efforts on developing the existing Maltby colliery to its full potential.

Thus YAC implemented a scheme to restructure the pit to handle an increased output by enlarging the screens and installing an aerial ropeway held aloft on tall pylons in order to carry spoil away to a large tip by means of a continuous succession of buckets transporting the waste material. These buckets were upended at various points along the aerial flight and the spoil heap grew as a series of conical hills which gradually increased in height subsequently burying the lower half of the pylons in spoil. In the 1940s the aerial ropeway was rebuilt and the pylons and cables dismantled and replaced with a different structure consisting of small buckets conveyed by an overhead gantry. The end of the gantry was periodically extended as the tip grew and ultimately the spoil heap would come to cover the site of Maltby Wood with one of the largest man-made hills in the country.

During the final years of the 1920s considerable strides were undertaken by YAC and in 1929 production finally exceeded pre-1923 levels and the colliery made its first profit since the First World War when £22,585 was recorded, although total losses since the start of trading had now amounted to £250,711. An unusual feature established in 1929 was the introduction of a pension scheme for the workforce following a similar scheme established at Denaby Colliery. On payment of 1s per week, the scheme would provide a pension of 30s for a married man or 20s a week for a single man on his retirement at 65, a very progressive development considering there was no state pension benefit provided at the time.

Before the First World War, an Albion Charabanc, registered C2627, was purchased by the colliery company, presumably to provide staff transport. In 1930 the Maltby Miners Home Coal & Transport Service Ltd. was established. This was an organisation perhaps unique in the country where the men of the pit had started their own bus company to provide pit buses to the colliery. Established by the

Maltby branch of the Yorkshire Miners' Association in 1930 and funded by a stoppage of 6d/week, the buses provided transport to Maltby Main Colliery from the various housing estates as well as from Tickhill and Edlington. Initially utilising a fleet of 6 second hand vehicles, including 2 from Sheffield Corporation, the company operated from a depot on Morrell Street; and it also owned a fleet of wagons for the delivery of the miners' concessionary coal.

As the colliery entered the 1930s, annual output was approaching 900,000 tons from a workforce of 2,645. Despite the onset of worldwide economic depression the successful development of Maltby Main continued and in 1935 the pit finally recorded an output above 1,000,000 tons per year produced by 2,749 men, its highest ever workforce. However, concerned with the national overproduction of coal and consequent drop in price from a flooded market, the Government, empowered by the Mines Act (1930), imposed a quota system on every colliery in the country which lead to considerable hardship in many of the country's mining districts. Maltby Main was allocated a standard tonnage of 1,074,468 tons per year. Production above this figure would be met by severe financial penalties with any over-production being deducted from the following year's allocation. The implementation of this ruling couldn't have come at a worse time for Maltby Colliery as it was looking to produce over 1,000,000 tons per year on which it could draw a significant profit. To avoid exceeding their standard tonnage allowances, many collieries reduced their output by dismissing many of their workforce or implementing a 3 or 4 day week. This obviously had the effect of bringing extreme hardship into many colliery communities during the 1930s.

However, in 1935, Maltby Colliery sought to exploit a potential loophole in the quota system legislation. By purchasing another colliery and instantly closing it down, the standard tonnage of the purchased pit could be added to that of the parent colliery. Several of the directors of Denaby Colliery also served on the boards of Strafford Collieries Ltd. and The Darton Main Colliery Company Ltd., owners of two small collieries in Barnsley. Therefore, they were able to ensure that Maltby Colliery could purchase the entire share capital of these companies for £65,000 with little opposition. Thus the standard tonnage of 146,665 and 125,605 allocated to Strafford and Darton respectively was added to the Maltby standard tonnage, permitting them to produce 1,346,738 tons at the Maltby shafts.

Whilst this arrangement benefitted the Maltby community which consequently didn't experience the extreme hardship of some of the surrounding mining districts in the 1930s, it proved disastrous to the miners and their families at Strafford and Darton who suddenly found themselves redundant and their collieries abandoned, despite the fact that a significant investment in a large housing estate of 200 colliery owned homes had been completed at Darton in 1926. With what now seems like ruthless efficiency, such was the potential for Maltby Main Colliery to produce extensive profits, it seems remarkable that other collieries and their communities could be sacrificed in order to serve this economic need. Since 1927, YAC had actually spent a total of £385,000 in developing Maltby Colliery in order to reach its full potential, potential which was finally realised in the second half of the 1930s when YAC was incorporated as a department of Amalgamated Denaby Collieries Ltd. in 1936.

Two motorbuses belonging to Maltby Miners Home Coal & Transport Service Ltd captured by an unknown photographer in the colliery yard, possibly photographed on the first day of operation. An initial fleet of 1925 vintage Bristol 4-ton motorbuses was purchased second hand from Sunderland & District Omnibus Company Ltd in 1930 and two of these five vehicles are shown here, including PT 4710. These vehicles were painted in a maroon and cream livery and the company continued in operation until the manpower reductions in the late 1990s. Today the bus depot on Morrell Street is used by a tyre company who have retained the fine wrought iron Maltby Miners Company sign above the former depot entrance. (Maltby Main Colliery Jubilee Brochure)

Prior to the 1930s, the concept of pit head baths was largely unknown as it was the norm for miners to wash in a zinc bath in front of the fire at home. Indeed most houses built before the First World War did not have an upstairs bathroom as this was an idea that was generally introduced into housing during the 1920s. However, one of the first pithead baths in the country was provided at Maltby Main Colliery in 1925. Nevertheless, the baths were initially underused as many colliers preferred to wash at home and save the 6d/week fee and it was not until 1939 that larger pithead baths with accommodation for 2,000 men were provided at the pit. These baths, designed by notable architect W. A. Woodland and built on concrete stilts, were connected undercover to the lamp room and by a covered gantry to the pithead for convenience.

Following the extensive investment in developing the pit together with the purchase of Strafford and Darton's standard tonnage allowance, for five consecutive years, Maltby produced over 1,000,000 tons and finally recorded healthy profits for its owners. With the outbreak of war, the quota system and depression of the 1930s ended and the colliery was encouraged to maintain maximum production to assist with the war effort. However, despite mining being a protected occupation, many of the men enlisted causing a labour shortage and consequently war time production dropped to around 700,000 tons per year from a workforce of 2,300. The national need for coal during the Second World War was addressed by the government in 1943 when they introduced numerous unskilled employees into the coal industry, for example 'Bevin boys' conscripted from the army, who lived in large army huts in the Rotherham Road area. Despite the fact that they had been conscripted into the mines, the Bevin boys made a significant contribution to the nation's war effort, however their overall lack of experience may have contributed to the fact that during the 1940s Maltby Colliery suffered from an unfortunate high number of fatalities such that the pit gained the unfortunate nickname 'the widow maker'.

Following the declaration of peace, the long hoped for nationalisation of the coal industry occurred on the 1st January 1947 and the National Coal Board (NCB) took over the management of Maltby Main Colliery. By way of compensation, Amalgamated Denaby Collieries was paid £5,721,200 for their pits at Maltby, Dinnington, Rossington, Denaby and Cadeby. Subsequently, Amalgamated Denaby Collieries and its subsidiary, the Maltby Main Colliery Company, were dissolved and wound up.

Although the story of the colliery in nationalised hands remains out of the scope of this publication, it is summarised in the following paragraphs.

The NCB immediately looked at ways to modernise and mechanise coal production at Maltby Colliery. Prior to 1944, coal had been mined by pick and shovel and transported to the pit bottom by 13cwt capacity tubs hauled by a combination of endless rope haulage and pit ponies. The first signs of mechanisation had occurred in 1944 when a conveyor system was introduced at the coal face to facilitate the loading of coal. However, the main problem stalling further mechanisation was the fact that the Barnsley seam dipped away from the pit bottom in all directions. By a geological quirk, the shafts had been sunk to the crest of an anticline, a shallow dome structure which meant that coal was hauled up a gradient in all directions to the pit bottom, making it impossible to introduce locomotive haulage.

During the annual pit holiday, the pit ponies were brought out of the colliery to enjoy their own holiday in the fields adjacent to Scotch Spring Lane where they have been captured in this interwar photograph. In the background can be seen the 6 houses forming 'Mechanic's Row' comprising the hamlet of Scotch Springs with the signal box on the SYJR on the right controlling the entrance to the colliery sidings. In one of these houses was born 'Firey' Fred Trueman, the Yorkshire and England international cricketer. Fred's father lived at 5 Scotch Springs and was the colliery ostler, responsible for the welfare of the ponies, and it may be him who is pictured with the wagon delivering feed on the right. The houses were cleared in the 1970s and this area was used as an extension to the colliery spoil heap. (Photographer Unknown - Thomas Best Collection)

To overcome this, the NCB decided to implement a reconstruction scheme at a cost of £3,000,000 from 1947-1961 in order to secure the life of the colliery as a high volume production unit. These plans called for deepening the shafts by 50 yards to a new winding level with the construction of a new pit bottom. This allowed the construction of 7,500 yards of new level roadways to the mining districts and the introduction of powerful diesel and electric battery locomotives hauling 4 ton capacity mine cars which replaced the rope and pony hauled 13 cwt capacity tubs. In 1954, coal cutting machines were introduced at the coal faces which fed conveyor belts loading directly into the mine cars. In 1961 the No.2 headgear was replaced with an electrically powered Koepe winding tower with skip winding where the coal is transported up the shaft in large capacity 12 ton skips rather than individual tubs. Electric winding was also introduced at the No.1

shaft with the installation of a new electrically driven Markham engine replacing the original Markham steam winding engines.

In 1968-1971 a further scheme was implemented at a cost of £1,250,000 to replace falling output in the Barnsley seam which by 1972 was exhausted after 61 years of continuous working. In 1970, the No. 1 shaft was deepened to the Swallow Wood seam (894 yards) and Haigh Moor seam (901 yards). Exploitation of these new reserves ensured that Maltby produced above 1,000,000 tons in 1973. On the surface a new coal preparation plant and rapid loading bunker was built to handle the increased output. The aerial ropeway was dismantled and replaced by a covered conveyor as the increased mechanical working of coal led to increased amounts of spoil and waste material. The spoil heap, once described by Thomas Best as "Maltby's mountain with its ski lift to the top" (the aerial ropeway representing the ski lift), was increasing in volume by a rate of 250,000 tons per year and it would eventually come to dominate the view from the villages of Braithwell and Stainton.

Following the two reconstruction schemes, coal output was maintained throughout the 1960s and 1970s at around 900,000 to 1,000,000 tons per year with the use of increasing mechanisation. This had the effect that Maltby coal was produced at a very competitive and economical rate and the pit eventually became one of NCB's most profitable mines. However, the colliery was having less and less influence on the local community due to the effects of mechanisation resulting in a gradual decrease in the levels of manpower. Having once employed a maximum of 2,749 men in 1934, the number gradually fell over the succeeding decades; to 2,000 by the early 1960s and 1,500 by the early 1980s. Further reductions following the National Strike of 1984 saw the number employed fall beneath the 1,000 level during the early 1990s. This was coupled with a gradual increase of the age profile of the workforce. As neighbouring collieries closed, some of their workforce transferred to Maltby Colliery, resulting in a reduction in the recruitment of local school leavers and apprentices. To counteract this, Maltby Urban District Council had been very progressive in attracting other forms of employment to Maltby to provide job opportunities for the local community. This policy had commenced during the Second World War with the opening of the Royal Ordnance Factory and continued on a smaller scale throughout the following decades. A noticeable development was the establishment of a knitwear factory to target female unemployment.

In 1981, a major project to extract the Parkgate coal seam at a depth of 1050 yards was approved by the NCB. Maltby Colliery was earmarked for a new No. 3 shaft dominated by a huge overhead reinforced concrete winding tower which became a local landmark. The tower housed two 4000 horsepower electric motors which hauled coal up the shaft using the 'Koepe' principle, equipped with four 25 ton skips in two pairs attached to one continuous cable running up and down the 26 feet diameter shaft. Coal was transferred to a new coal preparation plant for washing and screening before being conveyed to a large rapid loading bunker, purposely built to load continually moving 'merry go round' coal trains to supply the power stations of the Central Electric Generating Board, by now the largest consumer of coal in the country. This development would enable the pit to be developed as a high volume low cost unit capable of producing 2,500,000 tons per year. This work was finally completed in 1988 with the introduction of 'retreat mining' which permitted production to approach 2,000,000 tons during the 1990s. The colliery spoil heap had now reached a considerable height and the covered conveyor belt was subsequently dismantled, spoil now being tipped into the worked out limestone quarries at Stainton.

In 1993, the privatisation of British Coal, the successor to the National Coal Board, was announced and in 1994 Maltby Colliery together with the remainder of most of the assets of British Coal was purchased by RJB Mining for £815,000,000. Prior to 1994 RJB Mining, under its chairman Richard Budge, had been the largest independent mining operation in the UK and was based a few miles away at Harworth near Doncaster. By the turn of the millennium Maltby Colliery employed 1237 men who produced an annual output of 2,000,000 tons of coal. The main customer for this coal was West Burton Power Station in the Trent Valley and the Monckton coking plant near Barnsley.

In February 2007, Hargreaves Services Ltd. from County Durham purchased Maltby Colliery in a £30,000,000 deal from UK Coal, the successors to RJB Mining. One of the main reasons for the purchase was that Hargreaves could control their own supply of coal to their Monckton coking plant near Barnsley; this would claim 25% of the output. Of the remainder 60% was provided under a new contract to supply Drax Power Station near Goole. Under new ownership, the future of the colliery looked to be assured into the 21st Century. However, in May 2012 unusual and dangerous geological conditions were discovered that would ultimately lead to the closure of the colliery in 2013 with the redundancy of the remaining 540 employees, although some gained work with Hargreaves other South Yorkshire colliery at Hatfield. At Maltby, most of the surface buildings were demolished in 2014 with the cleared site ultimately earmarked for light industrial uses.

In 6th April 2013 a moving ceremony was held to mark the closure of Maltby Colliery when Kevin Barron MP, local union officials and hundreds of miners and villagers paraded behind the Miners Welfare brass band from the pit gates to the Grange Lane cemetery. There a ceremony was held which concluded with the burying of a lump of coal next to the grave of the unknown miner from the 1923 pit disaster. At the time of writing, the Maltby Miners Memorial Community Group hope to locate a memorial site on High Street to commemorate the 163 men who lost their lives whilst working at Maltby Colliery. The memorial will consist of the repositioning of the pit wheel and the cast iron 1908 date stone from the old pit gates, together with two mine tubs, a new 2013 date stone to mark the closure of the colliery and information plaques.

With the closure of Maltby Colliery, there now only remains in operation three deep mined collieries in the country, at Hatfield near Doncaster, Kellingley near Pontefract and Thoresby Colliery in Nottinghamshire, the latter two with an uncertain future at the time of writing.

The entrance to Maltby Colliery on Tickhill Road photographed in 2014. Later that year the date stone and pit wheel were removed for restoration by the Maltby Miners Memorial Community Group with the aim of repositioning them in a new site in High Street in 2015.

The Mining Community

An idea of the rural and picturesque nature of Maltby prior to the development of the colliery can be gathered from this view of the junction of Makin's Hill and Blyth Road, featuring the natural limestone spring known as The Well. Indeed, such was the attractiveness of the village and its surroundings that in 1907, readers of the Leeds & Yorkshire Mercury voted Maltby one of the Top 50 prettiest villages in Yorkshire. In the 1920s extensive road widening of Blyth Road running across the picture behind the well saw Makin's Hill converted into a stepped pedestrian access leading to High Street. The well has since disappeared beneath the entrance to Butler's Yard although the two cottages remain, the one on the left, possibly the oldest cottage in Maltby. (Edgar Scrivens Postcard c1908)

In 1901 the population of Maltby was 716 most of whom lived in a series of attractive stone built cottages with roofs of orange pan-tiles all clustered around a series of natural springs on the north side of the valley of Maltby Dike. At the centre of the village stands an old cross at the junction of the former Tinsley and Bawtry turnpike and the Rotherham to Barnby Moor turnpike. Therefore the village was of some importance to passing trade along these roads, catered for by three inns - The Don John, The White Swan and The Scarbrough Arms - together with a couple of informal tea or refreshment rooms as the village had become something of a picturesque stopping point for visitors to the ruins at Roche Abbey. Several of the cottages were owned as 'summer retreats' or let during the summer months to families from the industrial towns of Sheffield and Rotherham who wished to escape the hustle and grime of the city for the summer to enjoying the rural surroundings of the area with its waterside meadows and the natural rock outcrops that formed Maltby Crags on Wood Lee Common. The village with its small national school, post office and medieval church was overlooked by Maltby Hall, in which lived Lady Mabel Smith, the sister of Earl Fitzwilliam of Wentworth Woodhouse near Rotherham. In 1901, Maltby had become a civil parish with Rotherham Rural District Council and the West Riding County Council responsible for the area's local governance.

Already signs of change were beginning to affect the old village. In 1905 a small temporary tin town was established a mile away to the east, adjacent to where the SYJR intersected Blyth Road. This settlement was built to house the navvies working on the railway, although several took up lodgings in some of the cottages in the old village and all looked to the services of Maltby, notably the shops and pubs. In 1908 a second temporary tin town was established at Maltby Colliery to house the sinkers. Again the sinkers looked to Maltby for their services and the village school became overcrowded until the West Riding Education Authority provided a tin school in the pit yard for the sinker's children. However, the two tin towns were temporary settlements and on the opening of the SYJR in 1909 the navvies' tin town was dismantled and, following the completion of the sinking of the colliery shafts in 1911, the sinkers and most of their tin town moved to Rossington Colliery. However, it is possible that several of the huts saw further use in the model village: for example as a Salvation Army hut on Coleridge Road and as a fore runner of the Miners Institute on McConnel Crescent.

The announcement of the development of a colliery intended to employ over 3,000 men ensured that a massive housing scheme would be required to accommodate the workers and their families together with the numerous shops and services that would be needed to support what was essentially the provision of a new town. Initial correspondence between Maltby Main Colliery and the Sandbeck estate over the location of the village had centred on a possible site either side of Grange Lane or to the north of Tickhill Road, equidistant between the colliery and the old village, but still separated from the latter by agricultural land. At their Derbyshire operations, the Sheepbridge Company had worked with speculative builders over the provision of colliery housing and a contractor, Mr Green of Whittington, visited Maltby in the autumn of 1908 to look at possible sites for the colliery village on land belonging to Lord Scarbrough.

Whilst these negotiations were underway, a parallel proposal was drawn up by a syndicate headed by Maltby builder Herbert Mollekin and local landowner William Morrell over proposals for a colliery village on a 40 acre site to the north of Maltby Crags, bounded by High Street, Muglet Lane, Blyth Road and Millindale. This site was on an area of land still under private ownership, an area which had not yet either been leased to, or purchased by Maltby Main Colliery. However, following discussions with the syndicate, the colliery company purchased this site in December 1908 and contracted builder Herbert Mollekin to construct a 'model village' of miners' "cottages" (the term used for industrial housing at the time) to an overall plan drawn up by colliery company and which would be designated as Maltby Model Village. Under the contract drawn up with Herbert Mollekin, the colliery would guarantee the rental payments of the houses, whether occupied or not, with construction finances provided by mortgages raised by the builder. The Morrell name has been long connected with farming in the Maltby area and several branches of the family were engaged in this activity, either as tenant farmers or small holders. What is not clear is whether William Morrell is the same Mr Morrell who sold 31 acres of land to the colliery company in 1903, although possibly not, given his involvement in the syndicate who were possibly holding out to gain a better price from the colliery company. Nevertheless, the name Morrell was subsequently recorded for posterity when it was given to the longest street in the model village.

Hebert Mollekin, of Blyth Road, was a builder with a workforce of 250 men and he had been contracted to provide the housing at Dinnington Colliery in 1904/5 and had therefore worked with the Sheepbridge Coal & Iron Company at Dinnington. Mollekin had just completed a housing scheme for nearby Silverwood Colliery at Dalton, and was currently employed in providing housing for Grimethorpe and Frickley Collieries near Barnsley. These contracts were just about to come to an end so it was rather fortuitous that the Maltby Model Village scheme came to fruition in his own back yard.

There had been recent public and media condemnation as to the standards of colliery housing provided in certain areas, notably that provided at Denaby and Cadeby Collieries which had come under criticism for its use of uninspired monotonous rows of cramped terraced housing arranged in a grid iron pattern with the bare minimum of facilities, little recreational space and limited provision for amenities and gardens. This was coupled with the fact that several large collieries were rapidly developing around the Doncaster area all at the same time, all in competition with each other to attract a workforce which could possibly be swayed by the standard of the company owned housing. Further to this was a growing awareness of the Garden City Movement, a principle designed to enhance the provision and layout of industrial housing by the provision of what were known at the time as model villages, in that they were the ideal model of the very latest concepts in town planning. Brodsworth Colliery had constructed Woodlands

Model Village to the north of Doncaster, which had shown the way in what could be provided, and in 1908 Maurice Deacon drew up plans for a model village for Maltby Colliery.

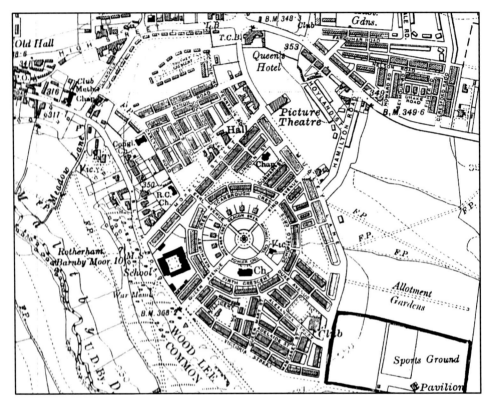

Maltby Model Village from the Ordnance Survey map of 1930. The prominent circular structure at the centre of the model village can be clearly seen and the layout is explained further in the text. (Crown Copyright Reserved).

A scheme for a self-contained model village was designed with an unusual layout consisting of a series of concentric circles and spokes, said to resemble a colliery winding wheel. This whole circular structure would sit within the centre of a triangular shaped piece of land bounded by three roads: the pre-existing Blyth Road and Muglet Lane plus a new road laid to the northwest of the site (connecting Blyth Road with Muglet Lane) and called Morrell Street after William Morrell, the original landowner. Of the roads forming the triangle, Morrell Street would be bounded by a strip of land designated for shopping facilities provided by private enterprise. Muglet Lane would face a mixture of open space, countryside, allotments and the sports grounds that accompanied the Miners Institute; whilst the houses fronting Blyth Road would face attractive southerly views over the open countryside of Maltby Crags and Wood Lee Common with Maltby Dike running in the valley below.

The central area would contain a bandstand surrounded by a public park. This would be in turn enclosed by a circle containing a series of large villas for colliery officials together with a site allocated for a new church and parsonage. This circle would be in turn surrounded by a second larger outer circle fronted with terraced housing for miners. Long straight terraced rows facing outwards would front the three sides of the triangular road network that bounded the site. The irregular shaped gaps contained between the larger triangle and the smaller circle would be allocated to further housing, in small streets with sites designated for schools, a Primitive Methodist chapel, a Miners Institute and several green spaces or squares. Radiating out from the central bandstand like spokes of a wheel were four avenues that independently linked up with the roads forming the triangle. Thus a striking and unusual layout was designed for Maltby Model Village

Construction commenced in 1909 as it was hoped to have the houses ready to be occupied for when the colliery came into production. A source of clay was located a mile to the west of old Maltby village and a brickyard was opened by the Maltby Metallic Brick Company to supply the building operations. Throughout the following years, a constant procession of traction engines and horse and carts hauled the bricks from the brickyard to a temporary stockyard in the central circle.

During 1910 building was well underway and the northern quarter was completed first comprising Lincoln Street, Durham Street, Scarbrough Crescent and Deacon Crescent where 3 large semi-detached villas were built. These villas each provided a superior standard of accommodation and consisted of a kitchen, scullery, living room and bathroom downstairs with three bedrooms upstairs. A fourth bedroom was contained within the attic storey with a window in the gable. These properties were provided with large gardens and outhouses and were designated for colliery over-men. They fronted the park and bandstand and were built for a cost of £250 each. During 1911 and 1912, the remainder of the village was completed including the four villas for deputies on McLaren Crescent. Although they were outwardly similar to the villas on Deacon Crescent, the internal accommodation was smaller.

The standard miners' cottages were provided in terraced groupings of various lengths, with terraces of 3, 4, 5, 6, 7, 8, 9, 10, 12, 14 and 16 houses. The whole development consisted of three different types of houses which were dependent upon the tenants' family circumstances:

Type 1 Cottage: 13 foot frontage. Parlour, kitchen and pantry in the main body of the house downstairs with a coal house and toilet contained within a projecting extension to the rear. Three upstairs bedrooms, one of which is carried over the projecting part of the lower storey. A small walled front garden with a porch over the front door and a yard to the rear. Above the front bedroom window a small gable was provided to break up the roof line. Rent: 6s6d per week.

Type 2 Cottage: 17 foot frontage. Same provision as Type 1 but this time the rooms were larger and contained within the body of the house, so there is no need for the projecting extensions of the house to the rear or the front porch, the advantages gained being that all window have full access to light and sunshine. Rent 6s9d: per week.

Type 3 Cottage: 23 foot frontage. A much larger property with rooms either side of a front door and 4 bedrooms upstairs. Rent: 7s per week.

This Edgar Scrivens postcard can be dated to 1910 when it was featured in a special report in the 29th July 1910 issue of The Doncaster Chronicle entitled The Minerals of Maltby. The northern quarter of the model village was the first to be completed including the large properties of Deacon Crescent with the smaller Type 2 cottages of Scarbrough Crescent behind. The latter were sometimes known as Sinkers Row, being the first houses finished in the model village and possibly occupied by some of the pit sinkers who chose to stay and embark on new careers at Maltby Colliery. The potato fields in the foreground would soon be built over with the laying out of McLaren Crescent and Hayhurst Crescent in 1911. (Brian Brownsword Collection).

All the houses were provided with a downstairs bath and a tap in the scullery that supplied water piped from the borehole in the colliery yard. The kitchen contained a Yorkshire range and a 'copper pot' for cooking and washing. Behind the properties ran a service or back lane, typically catering for the delivery of concessionary coal and the collection of household refuse which was rather unceremoniously tipped into a quarry on Maltby Crags in the early days. Rotherham Rural District Council was responsible for a sewage system that piped waste material to a large settling tank near Maltby Common. Gas lamps illuminated the street, fuelled with gas from the newly established Maltby & Bramley Gasworks near Hellaby Bridge, until 1923 when it was replaced by mains gas piped directly from the coking plant at Dinnington Colliery.

The centre of the model village was provided with a circular park containing lawns and gardens, and surrounded with privet hedges and iron railings with an ornate cast iron bandstand in the centre, as shown in this Edgar Scrivens postcard from 1911 with the Type 2 cottages of Schofield Crescent in the background. Of note is the temporary tin structure on the left positioned on a piece of land between Schofield Crescent and McConnel Crescent. This is possibly one of the original sinkers huts repurposed for further use in the model village, in this case to form the first Miners' Institute, prior to the opening of the permanent premises on Muglet Lane in 1914. Whether this hut saw further use elsewhere in the model village is unknown; it had disappeared from this location by the mid-1920s. To the right behind the bandstand the Parsonage was built in 1912 to house the incumbent of the Church of The Ascension. During the Second World War, the iron railings and bandstand were removed and melted down to assist with the war effort and fields of wheat were grown in the park. The whole area was later transformed in the 1970s with the demolition of the Parsonage and the covering of the park, McConnel Crescent, and Fowler Crescent (the latter two now disappearing and joining the lost street names of Maltby), with an estate of pensioners' bungalows, thus sadly ruining the overall concept of Maurice Deacon's centrepiece for Maltby Model Village. In the 1950s, a replacement bandstand was proposed by Maltby Urban District Council (MUDC) on a new site, but unfortunately it was never finished and its large concrete base remains in isolation in Maltby Crags Meadows.

The model village was completed with the distinctive naming of the streets. The inner circle of Deacon Crescent, McLaren Crescent, Fowler Crescent and McConnel Crescent were named after the directors of the colliery company. The outer circle represented the major landowners of the coal royalty: Scarbrough Crescent after Lord Scarbrough of Sandbeck, Hayhurst Crescent after the Reverend William France-Hayhurst of Wilsic Hall near Wadworth, Firth Crescent after Edward Firth, a member of the Sheffield Steelworks owning Firth family and landowner at Maltby; and finally Schofield Crescent, named after the Schofield family who owned Maltby Hall. The four avenues received the generic names of King Avenue, Queen Avenue, Duke Avenue and Earl Avenue (the latter unusual in that due to the layout of the houses, none have the address of Earl Avenue). Other smaller streets were named after members of the British royal family: Victoria Street, Albert Street, Alexandra Street and Adelaide Street (Adelaide being William IV's Queen. Additionally, two British cathedrals provided their names for Durham and Lincoln Streets, which leaves Margaret Street and Millicent Square, possibly named after other minor Royal family members.

King Avenue in the model village lined with newly completed Type2 cottages. Several improvements in the standard of colliery housing can be discerned from this picture, notably the width of the actual street itself, a vast improvement over the cramped streets of colliery housing provided elsewhere in the country only a few years earlier. The overall 'neatness' of the houses themselves is apparent, constructed with red brick and blue slate roofs, with dark green painted doors and windows, all set behind small front gardens. Architectural features of note include the provision of dormer roofs above the bedroom windows, the triangular area thus created finished in roughcast cement and painted white, with vertical wooden beams. Above the lower storey windows and below the upper storey windows, a prominent brick band was carried along the full length of each block. Subsequent renovation projects have seen many of the houses retiled with the dormer roofs and chimneys removed, but it is clear that some considerable thought went into the overall design process of the original housing provision.

Model Village Housing Contrasts:
Upper: *The smallest properties consisted of the Type 1 cottages complete with their neat front porches, as illustrated on this 1913 James Simonton postcard of Durham Street.*
Lower: *The largest properties consisted of these semi-detached officials' villas, as shown in this 1925 Edgar Scrivens postcard of Deacon Crescent and McLaren Crescent which faced the central park and Bandstand (John Petch Collection)*

Thus it can be seen that some considerable attempt and thought went into providing a quality standard of housing, both internally and in the overall layout of the model village, and the whole provision is a remarkable achievement considering the cottages were built for around £150-£160 each. By 1912, 552 properties had been built and occupied, consisting of 292 Type 1 houses, 218 Type 2 houses, 28 Type 3 houses (mostly around Millicent Square) and 14 houses for colliery officials. The first miners and their families had moved into the model village in 1910, subsequently christening their new home as "t'model" and on the 20th May 1911 a new branch of the Yorkshire Miners' Association was formed to represent the men ready to embark on a new life at Maltby Main Colliery.

There definitely must have been some sort of community spirit in the early days as 552 families from all over the country suddenly found themselves living and working in close proximity to each other in a model village created as a contemporary reflection of an industrial housing scheme influenced by the Garden City Movement principles of the day. Certainly the circular hierarchical layout is striking with the houses increasing in size as you move towards the centre circle, and looking back over a 100 years later, it is fair to say that the scheme had been a partial success and the colliery company were obviously proud of what they had achieved at Maltby. However, perhaps the real purpose of the model village was revealed by Maurice Deacon as a possible means to control his new workforce. Speaking in 1911 at a garden fete held to raise money for the model village church, Maurice Deacon spoke about his new creation and his new employees. He stated that since he was the one responsible for disturbing the beautiful Yorkshire countryside, his company desired to see "that the new population of miners should be as little objectionable as possible to the district." He stated that the Company had put itself to the expense of providing a village which they hoped would have the effect of making the colliers they employed as civilized and respectable as it was possible to be. He felt that "in the main the British collier was a proper and right-thinking individual who only wanted the guidance of those around him to lead the kind of life he really desired, a life of quietness and respectability."

Maurice Deacon's speech, when read today, can certainly be viewed as patronising to his workforce, but perhaps it should be recognised that it represents the views of a different era when there was this certain distinction between the master and his workers. However, Maltby Model Village does represent an achievement in the town planning ideals of the day and the standard of housing with the associated churches, chapels, schools, institute, bandstand and recreational space was much better than that provided at many earlier colliery settlements. It is a shame that this standard wasn't sustained in the succeeding extensions over the following few years with the creation of the company owned Admirals' estate and Poets' estate.

In 1912, Maltby Main Colliery was undergoing rapid expansion and a further housing development was commissioned from Herbert Mollekin on a site to the north of Tickhill Road. Unlike the distinctive circular plan of the model village, this development was arranged on a traditional grid plan and 173 houses were laid out on Farquhar Road, Nelson Road, Howard Road, Seymour Road, Drake Road, Fisher Road, Beresford Road all named after British Navy admirals, accounting for the area's later name of the Admirals' estate. In addition, the houses fronting Tickhill Road were originally known as Anston Terrace, but this may have been a misspelling of Anson, as there was an Admiral Anson. Whichever, Anson or Anston Terrace has now became one of Maltby's lost street names, its name now passing from memory.

Despite the caption of this 1913 James Simonton postcard reading Seymour Road, this is actually now Howard Road in the Admirals' estate with the houses of Nelson Road in the distance. The photographer has captured a splendid scene apparently full of optimism as the first inhabitants gather for the camera having just moved into the area, many from Staffordshire, and all ready to embark on a new life in Maltby. Type 1 cottages are illustrated on the left with their distinctive shared porches and gables over the bedrooms (some pictured without porches although these were later added), all facing the rear of the houses off camera to the right on Seymour Road. Similar cottages in Nelson Road can be seen in the distance, although the one with the family standing in the front door is one of the larger Type 3 properties with rooms either side of the central door. In the 1980s a handful of houses in the Admirals' estate were demolished, including 12 Type 3 properties on Farquhar Road and 6 Type 2 houses on Fisher Road.

Altogether in the Admirals' estate 62 Type 1 houses were built, 58 Type 2 houses and 53 Type 3 houses. All of these were provided with small front gardens and large rear yards and the development contains a number of unusual 'half streets', with houses lining one side of the street, those on the opposite side actually being the rear of the properties lining the parallel street. The streets were arranged around an open space fronted by 6 officials' houses, identical to those in the model village, whilst on one side two large villas were provided for the colliery manager and under-manager. Thus the Admirals' estate comprised 181 properties, all under occupation by 1913. Despite its British Navy connections, this area is now colloquially known by the nickname 'Chinatown'.

However, the colliery was continuing to expand and more people were moving into the district with the resultant demand for more housing. This was answered in 1914 when building of the Poets' estate commenced to the northwest of Morrell Street as an extension to the original model village. The Poets' estate consisted of Carlyle Road, Burns Road, Coleridge Road, Tennyson Road, Byron Road and Southey Crescent, again laid out on a grid plan with back lanes. Most of this estate was built and occupied by 1916 when developments in the First World War saw a suspension of building activities with Byron Road half completed. Perhaps war time restrictions or interruptions caused a slight change in the planning of this development. In this estate, none of the smaller Type 1 houses were provided, thus there were 96 Type 2 houses and 12 Type 3 houses. Sporadic building recommenced in 1919 with the construction of 19 Type 4 houses to complete Byron Road. Although internally similar to Type 2 houses, the Type 4 houses differed from their pre-war cousins in that the end house of each row projected beyond the building line and was provided with a large front gable in an attempt to add variety. Finally in 1920 14 additional houses in blocks of 2 and 4 were built on Carlyle Road and Southey Road. These were larger properties more typical of interwar housing with hipped roofs. Thus the Poets' estate was provided with a total of 141 houses. Although Herbert Mollekin had constructed the model village, there is reference to the building contractors Messrs Hopkinson & Co. of Worksop being involved with the construction of Maltby Colliery housing at this time. Whether this is in collaboration with or as replacement for Mollekin remains unknown, although if the latter, this may account for the architectural differences with the houses of the Poets' estate when compared with the model village.

Apart from Herbert Mollekin, other speculative builders had also looked to gain from providing houses for the influx of workers to the district. However, such housing developments were only small scale and piecemeal on small parcels of land which could often only accommodate a single terrace, for example on sites in Millindale, High Street, Cross Street and Rotherham Road where at the latter, a group of terraces mostly housed workers at the brickworks. One of the largest of these speculative housing schemes was the building of 20 houses on Milton Street near Rotherham Road, the name deriving from the Peterborough estate of Earl Fitzwilliam. Additionally, there was some earlier speculative building in the Braithwell area when there was initially some uncertainty as to where to locate the pit shafts.

An example of one of the first families to move to the model village is provided by the Best family who came to Maltby in 1911 to take up residence in one of the officials' houses at 3 Deacon Crescent. George Best had previously worked in agriculture in the Selby area, but had moved to Cadeby Colliery in 1896 working his way up to the position of over-man prior to moving to Maltby. George had seven children including Tom and Joseph who both worked at Maltby Colliery with their father, but unfortunately Joseph had lost his life in the 1923 pit disaster. The family, devastated by this loss, decided to leave Maltby and move to one of the newly built officials' houses at Rossington Colliery. However, in 1930, Tom Best returned to Maltby and moved into 22 Byron Road paying a weekly rent of 9s6d and took up a job at the pit. Tom married a local girl Rhoda, who worked in service in one of the Morrell family farms at Roche Abbey and they subsequently had four children, Joyce, Derrick, Thomas and Rhoda, the latter two still living in Maltby at the time of writing. The family is pictured outside 22 Byron Road in this 1940s photograph taken by the family lodger. (Thomas Best Collection).

With the opening of the colliery, families migrated into the area so that the 1911 census recorded a population of 1700, nearly 1,000 more than 10 years previously.

Most of the families had moved to Maltby from the older industrial and mining areas of the UK, particularly from Northumberland, Durham and Derbyshire. A notable contingent from Staffordshire moved into the newly completed Admirals' estate on Tickhill Road, thus earning the estate's nickname of 'Chinatown', possibly because most of the inhabitants had previously worked in the Staffordshire potteries producing china. This varied population was augmented by many people of Irish descent and by local people who had previously worked in agriculture, all drawn to a life at the new pit with the promise of a relatively well paid job and a company owned house to live in. Thus, in the early days, a veritable mixture of accents must have been heard on the streets.

By 1921, the population numbered 7,657, an increase of nearly 6,000 in 10 years. Despite this tremendous growth, Maltby Main Colliery was looking to build further housing to accommodate an even larger workforce, but post-war inflation had ensured that construction costs had quadrupled compared to pre-war and housing costs were now taking up increasing amounts of capital. The Town Planning Act (1919) and the Mining Industry Act (1920) stated that housing had now to be built to higher standards. To address this, Maltby Colliery purchased 58 steel framed '*Dorlonco*' houses from Dorman Long & Company, the Middlesbrough based industrial concern. These unusual houses were built in pairs with a large steel framed structure with sections bolted together with steel lathing. The external walls were covered with concrete render, thus eliminating the use for expensive bricks. In doing this, the Dorlonco architects (which included notable town planner Sir Patrick Abercrombie) had created a well-proportioned house with large interior accommodation. At Maltby, 26 of the 58 Dorlonco houses were laid out along Southey Crescent, an extension to Southey Road in the Poets' estate, whilst the remainder fronted the south side of Millindale and High Street. Thus the whole area bounded by Millindale, High Street, Muglet Lane and Blyth Road was now enclosed with colliery housing which now adjoined the stone cottages of old Maltby, the old and new meeting along opposite sides of Millindale.

However, later structural problems would plague the steel frame and concrete render of several Dorlonco houses throughout the country resulting in their demolition (for example, all of the 74 supplied to Rossington Colliery were cleared in the 1970s). Fortunately for those at Maltby, the structural problems had been recognised early enough and in the 1940s the problem of the deteriorating steelwork was addressed and the concrete render was replaced with an outer brick skin, thus extending their lives, with the exception of a pair on High Street which were subsequently demolished.

The shortage of housing and the increased cost of providing such housing was a factor shared by many of the South Yorkshire collieries at this time and the only answer to the problem of increasing building costs would be for several of the Yorkshire and Derbyshire colliery companies to get together to form their own house building company. Thus in 1922, Maltby Main Colliery became one of the members of the Industrial Housing Association Ltd. (IHA) an organisation created under the guidance of Sir Tudor Walters representing The Housing & Town Planning Trust and Lord Aberconway representing the colliery companies. The advantages of scale ensured that bulk purchases kept the price as low as possible and that Government grants and loans could be accessed to help with the building costs.

At Maltby the IHA purchased two 40 acre sites to either side of Grange Lane with the intention of providing a large estate for Maltby Colliery. In 1922 work commenced on laying out the first site to the west of Grange Lane. The IHA provided houses arranged in blocks of 2, 3, 4, & 6 to a variety of designs and all provided with extensive gardens. The roads of this estate took the names of landed gentry; and Salisbury Road was laid out in 1922, followed by the building of Clarence Place, Devonshire Road, Norfolk Place and Portland Place in 1923.

A further IHA estate was planned for the eastern side of Grange Lane but the pit disaster of 1923 put paid to any further expansion plans and consequently only Haslam Place was built of the eastern development, taking its name from Thomas Haslam the Secretary to Maltby Main Colliery. In total the IHA provided 364 houses at a cost of approximately £450 each and all built to a high standard with a downstairs bathroom and three or four bedrooms upstairs. The estate also included two unusual developments of houses with low roofs and large dormer windows, 12 arranged around a square on Salisbury Road and 26 arranged around the eastern end of Devonshire Place. These were possibly designed by architect and builder Frederick Hopkinson of Worksop as they are identical to houses constructed in the early 1920s by Hopkinson for Hatfield Colliery in Stainforth.

Concurrently with the development of Maltby as a colliery settlement during the second decade of the 20th Century, Maltby Parish Council had been seeking urban powers in order to have a greater control over the affairs of the new village. An earlier application had been unsuccessful but had seen that part of Doncaster Rural Council containing the colliery site and Scotch Spring Lane become designated as Stainton Urban District. However, in 1924, a further application to the West Riding County Council saw the areas governed by Maltby Parish Council and Stainton Urban District being merged into a new district under the stewardship of Maltby Urban District Council (MUDC) which was eventually based at Maltby Grange on Rotherham Road. With newly awarded urban status, the council was granted with greater powers thus enabling it to access loans and subsidies to assist with the house building programme in the area. The new authority, under the leadership of Edward Dunn and Hughie Ross, seems to have been very progressive in wanting to become a major part of the growth of Maltby. Both Hughie Ross and Edward Dunn were employed as colliery check-weigh-men. They were prominent union officials and typical of a new breed of men that were looking to take the area forward for the benefit of the local community. In 1935 Edward Dunn was elected Labour MP for the Rother Valley constituency and his achievement in his civic duties both locally and nationally was subsequently recognised with the opening of the Edward Dunn Memorial Hall on Tickhill Road.

In 1922, Rotherham Rural District Council had purchased 18 areas of land from Edward Schofield of Maltby Hall and had commenced building 76 houses on various sites to the north of Rotherham Road. Part of this scheme entailed the compulsory purchase of several stone built cottages in order to facilitate the widening of Rotherham Road and Blyth Road and thus remove what was known as 'the bottleneck' at the western end of the old village. These 76 new houses were completed by the newly formed MUDC and some of these properties are shown lining Rotherham Road either side of the entrance to Rolleston Avenue. MUDC also added an estate of 36 houses on Rolleston Avenue, which took its name from George Rolleston, vicar of Maltby from 1816-1868 and owner of Maltby Hall at the time. MUDC added their first estate of 36 houses as an extension to Rolleston Avenue in 1926 (these are the houses with the lower storey in brick and the upper storey in white cement render seen in the distance in the above illustration). At a cost of £17,781 (just under £500 each) these 36 houses were designed by the MUDC's architect and built by Herbert Mollekin who provided a celebratory lunch at the Queens Hotel for members of the council. At this lunch, Herbert Mollekin addressed the concern of post war inflation when he stated that he had once provided houses for a cost of £135 each, but nowadays the bricks themselves cost that amount. (Postcard by Edgar Scrivens, c1932).

Millindale showing the dramatic transformation of a street. Upper view dates from 1908 with the lower illustration depicting the same location 15 years later, with stone cottages demolished to make way for street widening, and the construction of speculatively built brick terraces from 1911/2 and the unusual grey concrete steel framed Dorlonco houses built in 1920 (Both postcards photographed by Edgar Scrivens)

Grange Lane on a postcard from c1950 by James Simonton showing some of the houses provided by MUDC in the 1930s. In the distance are the houses provided by the Industrial Housing Association in the mid-1920s. Both of these later housing developments were built to a very high standard, once again employing local builder Herbert Mollekin and using Maltby metallic bricks.

Nevertheless, MUDC's first housing scheme had been built to a very high standard and was followed by further developments with the completion of 32 houses on the Herne Hill estate at Charnell Avenue in 1928 and 40 houses in Hamilton Avenue and Hoyland Street in 1929. However, on September 13th 1930, MUDC embarked on its largest housing scheme to date when it purchased a 40 acre site to the east of Grange Lane for the sum of £2,200 from the colliery in order to develop the Woodlands Estate.

This area had previously been earmarked for the development of more colliery owned housing constructed by the Industrial Housing Association, however, it seems that since the establishment of MUDC, the colliery company were more than happy for the local authority to take over the expense and responsibility of providing additional housing. By 1935, MUDC had built 393 houses on the Woodlands estate, surrounding the earlier housing provided by the IHA on Grange Lane and Haslam Place, enclosing Maltby Cemetery and linking up with the Admirals' Estate. During the early 1930s, Highfield Park, Ash Grove, Birchfield Road, Lime Grove, Heatherdale Road, Park View, Rosston Road and Dunns Dale were laid out with well-proportioned houses of two different designs, arranged in blocks of 2 and 4 with a solitary block of 3 on Grange Lane accounting for the final odd numbered figure of 393. Similar in nature to the earlier IHA housing on the western side of Grange Lane, the houses of the Woodlands estate were all equipped with a downstairs bathroom and 3 or 4 upstairs bedrooms. The pride of MUDC with this major housing scheme even extended to the naming of some of the roads, Rosston Road after Hughie Ross and Dunn's Dale after Edward Dunn.

In the 1930s, MUDC were keen to provide additional housing and they purchased the 147 acre Manor Farm estate to the north of High Street and formerly occupied by Mr. Morrell. In 1938, 118 houses in groups of 2 and 4 were laid out along Manor Road which connected Salisbury Road to High Street. This time, the bathrooms were provided upstairs. However, the outbreak of the Second World War interrupted any further building operations.

In 1931 the population of Maltby had increased to 10,010 most of whom relied on the colliery for their income. By the end of the 1930s when the pit was producing a million tons per year from a workforce of nearly 3,000 men, a grand total of 1,999 houses had been built in the following developments:

MMC Pit Yard and Scotch Spring Lane	**8**	**(1909)**
MMC Model Village	**552**	**(1910-1911)**
MMC Admirals' Estate	**181**	**(1912-1913)**
MMC Poets' Estate	**141**	**(1914-1915)**
MMC Dorlonco Houses	**58**	**(1920)**
MMC Industrial Housing Association	**364**	**(1922-1925)**
MUDC Rotherham Road Estates	**112**	**(1925-1926)**
MUDC Charnell Avenue	**32**	**(1928)**
MUDC Hamilton Road / Hoyland Street	**40**	**(1929)**
MUDC Woodlands Estate	**393**	**(1931-1934)**
MUDC Manor Road Estate	**118**	**(1937-1938)**

MMC denotes those houses under the control of Maltby Main Colliery (1,304) and
MUDC denotes those houses provided by Maltby Urban District Council (695)

The expanding mining population, housed in colliery-owned, council-owned or privately rented speculative built properties, created a new settlement which almost engulfed the earlier village. This meant that a whole host of services would be needed in the form of shops, schools, pubs, clubs, places of worship, and leisure facilities together with transport connections to surrounding towns. With the building of Maltby Model Village, allocation had been provided for a church, chapel, school and a Miners' Institute but the first need for the new populace would be shopping facilities as the conveniences provided in the old village would be totally inadequate.

In 1910 the first speculatively built shops opened on High Street, followed by a post office in 1911 near the Don John Inn. In 1912, a row of shops was built by private enterprise along Muglet Lane which included a branch of the Rotherham Co-operative Society and a prominent building belonging to Millard's. A further shopping area developed around the junction of Millindale and High Street which included a second branch of the Rotherham Co-operative Society adjacent to an area designated for use as Maltby Market containing several open air market stalls. (The area adjacent to The Swan Inn was occasionally referred to as Maltby Market but never functioned as a proper market as such). Smaller scale shopping facilities were provided along Morrell Street opposite the model village. In the 1920s and 1930s, the northern side of High Street was developed as more shops were built between the police station and Grange Lane (one prominent group of shops bears the date stone 1931) and along the south side of Tickhill Road opposite the Admirals estate.

Despite the initial optimism present when the first residents moved into the model village, life must have been hard with the outbreak of the First World War, colliery strikes in 1912, 1921 and 1926, the temporary closure of the pit following the 1923 disaster and the reduced workforce requirements during the Depression of the early 1930s. Many of the houses were overcrowded, one even containing a family of 15, and infant mortality and childhood illnesses was exceptionally high. During the 1920s and 1930s when the colliery was not working, the only form of financial income would be a small dole allowance or union strike pay and the villagers undoubtedly suffered tremendous hardship during these times. This picture possibly depicts the distribution of 'dole bread' during the 1921 strike and is taken in one of the classrooms of Crags School (Photographer Unknown, Thomas Best Collection).

In 1911, the Don John Inn was rebuilt as a new public house for the district but in the succeeding years, mining being thirsty work, the men preferred to drink in the Working Men's Clubs and the Miners Institute adjacent to the model village. Perhaps in recognition of the miner's reputation for enjoying his beer, the West Riding County Council opened a police station in 1912 on High Street and appointed the village constable 'Bobby' Lambton, to keep an eye on the inhabitants of the new village!

In 1914, the Maltby Main Colliery Institute Ltd was registered with a capital of £1,000 to build the Miners' Institute and run the facility on behalf of the colliery company. The subscribers to the capital included many Maltby residents together with Maurice Deacon, the colliery chairman. The Institute, more commonly known as "The 'Stute", opened on a site on Muglet Lane and replaced the earlier tin structure located near the bandstand. The new facilities included a cricket pitch with pavilion, bowling greens and a football ground for Maltby Main Football Club. This was formed in 1916 and its squad of players was drawn from the employees at the pit. Indeed it was said that a good footballer was guaranteed employment at the colliery so that his skills could enhance the reputation of the football club.

Edgar Scrivens returned to Maltby in the early 1930s to capture the growth of the town for a further series of commercial postcards and one such example is shown here, showing the newly completed Welfare Ground on Muglet Lane with a group of local miners enjoying a game of bowls. The park is overlooked by the rear of the MUDC houses of Hoyland Street and the ample size of these properties can be clearly seen.

The Mining Industry Act (1920) had seen the establishment of the British Miners Welfare Fund whose purpose was to improve the social well-being, recreational facilities and general conditions in the coalfields of the country. The fund gained its income from a levy of a penny on every ton of coal produced. In the late 1920s, under funding provided by the scheme, the Maltby Institute received improved sporting facilities and a new park containing bowling greens and tennis courts was created in the area between Hamilton Road and Muglet Lane on a site donated by the colliery company. This was designated as Muglet Lane Recreation Ground and opened in 1930 but was subsequently renamed Coronation Park in 1937 to mark the Coronation of King George VI.

In addition to the licensed premises in the old village and the institute in the model village, there were several working men's clubs established in the early days and one of the most popular was the Progressive Club adjacent to the Admirals' estate. This club eventually gained the nickname of The Slip, so called because the miners liked to 'slip in' for a pint or two on their way home from work. The working men's clubs were very popular and their number increased with the opening of the British Legion and the Catholic Club. This expanding market in beer sales attracted the national breweries, keen to get a share of this trade. Therefore in 1919, plans were drawn up for the opening of a new public house on Grange Lane to tap this demand and a large building was about to open as a pub when it was suddenly converted into five houses and a shop. However, in 1923,a large licensed premises was provided with the opening of the Queens Hotel by John Smiths Brewery at the cross roads formed by the junction of High street, Grange Lane, Tickhill Road and Muglet Lane. This intersection subsequently gained the name Queens Corner.

As well as the provision of shopping facilities and licensed premises, the education of the children of the new settlement would need to be addressed. Initially, the children of the sinkers residing at the tin town had walked to the national school in old Maltby village or the school in Stainton, until the opening of their own tin school in 1909. As the first families moved into the model village, the youngsters attended the tin school in the pit yard prior to the opening of the large Crags School on June 17th 1912, when they transferred to the new school and the tin school in the pit yard closed. The Crags School opened with a roll of 345 children, consisting of 119 infants, 108 junior girls and 118 junior boys. By 1921 the roll call had reached 1,470 and the school had become overcrowded and several wooden former First World War army huts had been acquired and positioned in the grounds for use as overspill classrooms. However, in 1922 to relieve pressure on the Crags School and provided for the interwar housing developments, the West Riding County Council purchased Maltby Hall and 18 acres of land from

Edward Schofield, subsequently demolishing the property and building a secondary school at a cost of £30,000 in the grounds which opened in 1926. In 1933, further reorganisation came with the opening of Maltby New Hall Infants' School adjacent to the Secondary School.

The Crags School pictured shortly after its opening in 1912 on this postcard by James Simonton. The school, provided by the West Riding Education Authority at a cost of £10,000 was splendidly situated adjacent to Maltby Crags and was named by the Doncaster Chronicle as "the first on the quadrangle principle and the finest in the country". Despite this heartening recommendation, by the early 21st Century the school was no longer considered fit for purpose and was demolished in 2005 being replaced by a new school on a different site, under the name of Maltby Crags Community School. (Brian Brownsword Collection)

However, the most prominent educational development occurred, after much campaigning by Edward Dunn, when on April 16th 1932, the West Riding County Council opened Maltby Grammar School on the site of Maltby Hall which offered scholarships to children from Maltby and the surrounding area; with 72 pupils enrolling in its first year. Further extensions to the Grammar School were built in 1938. In 1940, St Mary's Roman Catholic School opened in Muglet Lane providing education for Maltby's Catholic community. Plans for another school on the Maltby Manor Estate were drawn up in the late 1930s but were delayed by the outbreak of the Second World War, with Maltby Manor School finally opening in 1952.

As well as making provision for the educational needs of the new workforce, Maltby Model Village had also accommodated the spiritual needs of the new community as the church in old village with its small graveyard was considered inadequate. In February 1911, a local committee had been appointed for the purpose of assisting the South Yorkshire Coalfield Churches Extension Committee which had been formed in 1910 to serve the spiritual needs of the population of the new colliery villages of South Yorkshire. On a site donated by the colliery company the Committee constructed the Church of the Ascension at a cost of £2,500, which was dedicated on Ascension Day, 16th May 1912. The church, with a capacity of 400 worshippers, was built in a Romanesque or Lombardy architectural style and is nearly identical to those provided by the Committee at the colliery villages of Bentley, Edlington and Rossington. The Church was built from pressed Conisborough bricks and Kiveton Park limestone and includes decorative circular details in the brickwork and floor tiles reflecting the circular pit wheel layout of the model village. The first curate was the Reverend Douglas Crick who lived in the accompanying parsonage in the model village. The new church acquired a former First World War army hut for use as a church hall and placed this structure in the centre of Millicent Square. The church hall was used for numerous social functions until its dismantling in the 1960s.

The Church of the Ascension was built between Fowler Crescent and Firth Crescent on a site donated by the colliery company. Known as 'The Miners Church' the building was later provided with two fine stained glass windows. The Dufty memorial window portrays the Ascension and is in memory of Ernest Sydney Dufty, the son of the model village's first doctor, Ernest Emmanuel Dufty. The other window represents 'The Light of The world' and is in memory of the men who lost their lives in the Pit Disaster of July 28th 1923. In the 1990s, the church ceased functioning as a place of worship and was subsequently converted into residential apartments and the two windows were removed for safe storage. It is hoped that the windows may form part of a proposed new community building. (Postcard by Edgar Scrivens 1925).

Recognising the need for a burial ground to cater for the huge increase in population, in 1913 Maltby Parish Council purchased a 3 acre site in Grange Lane from Lord Scarbrough for use as a cemetery. In that year Lord Scarbrough offered Beech House in Blyth Road for use as a miners' cottage hospital which he hoped would be run and funded by a deduction from the colliers' wages. However, the outbreak of the First World War and the subsequent provision of hospital facilities at Rotherham saw this plan abandoned.

The model village also provided sites for places of worship belonging to other faiths. In 1911, the Primitive Methodists arrived from nearby Dinnington and acquired a wooden hut, possibly one of the huts used by the sinkers at the colliery, for use as a place of worship, and positioned this on a site between Lincoln Street and Durham Street. In 1915, this wooden hut was moved to Morrell Street where it became the Salvation Army Hall. It was replaced with a semi-permanent building, known as the tin tabernacle chapel. This building eventually became the colliery housing building maintenance depot. The Wesleyan Methodists had established a small stone built chapel in 1832 on Blyth Road. Rather than provide a new place of worship in the model village, they choses to greatly enlarge their existing premises in 1912 to cater for the new community which was within easy walking distance. In 1913, the South Yorkshire Coalfields Mission provided a wooden building for Maltby Congregational Church on Carlyle Road. However, this structure burnt down on Christmas Day 1925 and was replaced with a brick building dedicated on 2nd June 1927. Initially the Roman Catholic population had held their service in Herbert Mollekin's garage, but in 1914 they opened a wooden building on Morrell Street. This building served them well for 40 years until it was replaced by the present brick built structure. The stone laying ceremony for this was held on 5th August 1954 although the church was not actually consecrated until 6th May 1974.

The development of various recreational services for the new settlement continued throughout the 1910s and 1920s. The Maltby Main Brass band was formed in 1911 and the Globe Picture Theatre opened in 1913 on Carlyle Street as a cinema for the model village. One year earlier had seen the registration of The Maltby Picture Palace Ltd. which eventually provided a much larger cinema on Muglet Lane, possibly opening in 1920. For a time, such was the popularity of 'going to the pictures' that during the 1920s the model village benefitted from two cinemas before the Globe Theatre closed in 1930 and its premises became part of the Miners' Home Coal Delivery Service. Another popular interwar pastime was the playing of billiards and a billiard hall opened on High Street in the early 1920s. Many of the families of the model village had an allotment on a large site to the east of Muglet Lane where keeping pigs was popular. In the 1920s further allotments were established to the north of High Street to serve the families of the housing developments in the Grange Lane area.

Muglet Lane captured by postcard publisher Edgar Scrivens in 1925. The shops on the left were provided by private enterprise in 1912. The distinctive semi-circular frontage of Milliard's opened as a furniture store and the premises leant its name to a short extension of Byron Road called Milliard Lane. The Picture House on the right opened shortly after the First World War and was incredibly popular eventually trading as the Grand Cinema until changing fashions in the 1970s saw it converted for use as a bingo hall. Later the front of the building was remodelled and the interior converted into shop units which subsequently became vacant. The derelict building burnt down in 2013 and has since been demolished.

Maltby Model Village was constructed adjacent to Maltby Crags, where in 1924 Lord Scarbrough unveiled a war memorial built of grey Cornish granite on a site opposite the Crags School. In 1933, MUDC purchased the Crags Meadows (a series of meadows located between Maltby Crags and Maltby Dike) in order to develop leisure facilities for the people of Maltby. This included playing fields for recreational use and in 1935 the MUDC opened Maltby lido and an adjacent paddling pool. There were proposals for a Dance Hall, Bandstand and to dam the Maltby Dike to form a boating lake but these plans were never developed. Nevertheless, the Crags Meadows, Maltby Crags, Wood Lee Common and Maltby Low Common (the latter three being common land owned by the Sandbeck estate) all became a well-used recreational area for the miners and their families. The field on top of the crags was frequently used as a site for visiting fun fairs and the foot-

In 1925 photographer Edgar Scrivens captured the development of Maltby for the production of a series of commercial postcard views.
Upper: The Queens Hotel which occupied large premises on the Tickhill Road / Muglet Lane Junction with the photographer's car outside. (Brian Brownsword Collection)
Lower: Tickhill Road originally extended further westwards (hence the postcard caption) but this is now High Street showing the shopping facilities developed near the junction with Millindale.

path through the Crags Meadows from St Bartholomew's Church through the Norwoods to Roche Abbey was a particularly popular walk, especially on summer Sundays. Today the Crags, containing their natural limestone outcrops, have been designated a Regionally Important Geological and Geomorphological Site and, together with Wood Lea Common and Maltby Low Common (managed as a nature reserve by Yorkshire Wildlife Trust) this area now forms a Site of Special Scientific Interest.

Maltby's first swimming pool! In 1911, the miners of the Model Village dammed Maltby Dike to form an impromptu open air swimming pool as depicted in this James Simonton postcard in 1913 captioned 'In the Meadows' and featuring several youngsters bathing in the stream. The picturesque Crags Meadows, Maltby Crags and the valley of Maltby Dike became a popular recreational area. In 1935, MUDC constructed the open air lido on a nearby site to provide proper swimming facilities. (Brian Brownsword Collection).

The phenomenal growth of Maltby during the early 20th Century meant that the developing village would need transport links with the surrounding areas of population. At the time, a local carrier's horse drawn wagon provided a trip to Rotherham and Tickhill and a weekly departure to Doncaster Market but walking remained a popular activity. In 1909, Maltby Railway Station had opened on the SYJR at a location some distance from the village and this provided three daily departures to both Doncaster and Worksop. However, this service was withdrawn in 1929 when the SYJR became freight only apart from the occasional working men's club annual outing to the coast which departed in private hire trains from the old platforms.

On October 3rd 1912, a service of 'trackless trams', otherwise known as trolleybuses, was provided by Rotherham Corporation from Maltby to Broom where they connected with the Corporation's tram cars from Broom to Rotherham. However the Maltby terminus was on Rotherham Road, some considerable distance from the colliery and the model village, the bottleneck of older cottages prohibiting the eastwards extension of the trolleybus route. However, following road widening improvements, on 14th December 1924, the trolleybuses were extended along High Street to a terminus at Queens Corner.

Despite the postcard caption reading Tram Terminus, Maltby's first trolleybus service was provided on October 3rd 1912, when Rotherham Corporation purchased three Railess Electric Traction vehicles to operate what was then the longest trolleybus route in the country. This route operated from Broom to Rotherham Road in Maltby where fleet number 40 is depicted at the terminus in a splendidly rural setting, progression to the village centre prohibited by the narrowing of the road in the distance. The somewhat primitive solid rubber-tyred vehicle is pictured approximately where the Rotherham Road petrol station was later built, with the wall on the left forming the front garden wall of the Rotherham Rural District Council houses that were later completed by MUDC in 1925. The entrance to Rolleston Road is in the vicinity of the second pole on the left. (Postcard published by Edgar Scrivens c1914)

One of the first local bus services started in 1924 when East Midland Motor Services provided a new service from Dinnington via Thurcroft and Maltby and Edlington to Doncaster thus linking up several of the new colliery settlements with the market town. This was followed by a Sheffield to Maltby motor bus service operated jointly by Sheffield and Rotherham Corporations which provided transport links to the City and the industrial east end of Sheffield.

Thus, by the end of the 1930s, despite the economic situation at the time, Morrell Street had become the centre of model village life, ultimately containing the Labour Exchange, sub Post Office, Off Licence, Pawnbroker, several places of worship, three fish and chip shops, the pit bus depot and the Doctor's Surgery belonging to Dr Dufty who resided in a large villa constructed at the junction of Morrell Street and Blyth Road. Additional shops on Muglet Lane, Tickhill Road and High Street, together with Maltby Market, ensured that every need could be catered for by the shops of the town without the need to visit Rotherham and Doncaster. The Maltby Urban District Council had become a very progressive and forward looking local authority, responsible for numerous developments in what was now becoming a small town. The colliery had finally reached its full potential and was now producing over a million tons of coal per year.

During the Second World War, many of the men enlisted and to provide employment for some of the woman of the village, MUDC were successful in persuading the Ministry of Defence to build a Royal Ordnance Factory near the colliery. The workforce was augmented with families who moved to Maltby from the London area and to accommodate them a group of 120 unusual flat roofed houses were built in an estate to the north of Salisbury Road which became known as 'Little London'. The post-war growth of Maltby remains to be told elsewhere although it is summarised in the following paragraphs.

Following the nationalisation of coal mining industry in 1947, MUDC continued with an extensive building programme on the Manor Estate, completing the area to the east of Braithwell Road when the population was recorded as 12,448 in the 1951 census. Further MUDC housing schemes continued in the Cliff Hill and Addison Road area throughout the 1950s and 1960s. In the early 1970s MUDC developed the first part of the Birk's Holt estate on an area to the east of Muglet Lane. They planned and designed the second part of Birk's Holt but this was completed by Rotherham Borough Metropolitan Council (RMBC) after the local government reorganisation of 1974. Nevertheless, by the time of its absorption into RMBC in 1974, MUDC had built around 1,800 houses, an incredible achievement for such a small authority.

Its accomplishments were not limited to housing as MUDC had been very progressive in other areas, a notable development in the 1960s was the new precinct on High Street, consisting of Swimming Pool and Leisure Centre, Fire Station and Library. Finally, the Edward Dunn Memorial Hall opened as a community centre, named after the council's first Chairman. It is probably fair to say that since its dissolution in the 1974 local government reorganisation, MUDC has been much missed by the local population.

This superb scene of Maltby life in the 1950s has been recorded in this photograph of Queens Corner, the cross roads formed by the intersection of Grange Lane, Tickhill Road, Muglet Lane and High Street. In 1924, the Rotherham Corporation trolleybus service was extended to a new terminus adjacent to the Queens Hotel where 30 years later on 30th April 1954, David Packer photographed fleet number 12 (FET 612), a Daimler CTE6 trolleybus shown here having negotiated the turning circle. Behind the splendid West Riding County Council finger post and waiting on Grange Lane, can be seen a motorbus belonging to Maltby Miners Home Coal & Transport Service Ltd. This vehicle is an AEC Regal registered BVH 170, and purchased second hand from Huddersfield Joint Omnibus Committee. In later years, Maltby Miners became a very successful operation and was able to purchase its own fleet of brand new vehicles. (David Packer Collection Ref 178/153)

The post-war building programme was also contributed to by the NCB who provided an estate to the south of Tickhill Road known as White City, so called because the houses were assembled from ready-made concrete panels with a white cement render finish. Many of these houses were inhabited by miners from the older coalfields of Scotland and Northumberland whose collieries were closing at the time and they looked to transfer to the South Yorkshire Coalfield.

During the 1980s the National Coal Board was actively looking to reduce its housing stock and transferred most of its housing in Maltby to RMBC. Since then under the right to buy policy, many of the former pit houses have passed into private hands and private landlords, although a large proportion is still controlled by RMBC.

Building continued throughout the 1970s and 1980s with the provision of several private housing estates and Maltby was establishing itself as a popular commuter village, ideal for those working in the nearby towns of Rotherham, Doncaster and Worksop. By 1991, the population numbered 17,111 and the settlement has become a veritable small town. As the number employed at the colliery continued to dwindle throughout the latter half of the 20th Century, many people sought work outside the area, helped by the town's excellent links to the motorway network via the M18 and M1 motorways and its frequent public transport service to Rotherham.

On 31st May 2008, the village held a special gala day to mark the centenary of Maltby Colliery, but five years later the closure of the colliery was announced due to dangerous geological conditions. Today Maltby stands as a tribute to 20th Century coal mining development. The coming of the colliery was the catalyst in transforming a little village of stone cottages into a small town. Maltby awaits an uncertain future but a future that I am sure the local community has the strength to embrace.

Glossary

Barnsley Seam A highly prized seam of coal up to 10 feet thick within the Coal Measures of South Yorkshire which is only found at the surface near the town of Barnsley but lies buried at depth in the Doncaster area.

Bunker A large container used for the storage of coal before the coal can be treated in the screens and washery of a coal preparation plant.

Cage A steel structure used to transport men or coal filled tubs up and down the shafts. Some cages had two decks. The cage was attached by a steel rope to the winding engine.

Coal Measures A thick sequence of rocks and strata which consists of sandstones, shales, clays and coal seams. The coal measures of Yorkshire contain around 30 different coal seams.

Coal Preparation Plant A building where the treatment of coal is undertaken prior to dispatch, usually containing screens, washery and a conveyor leading to a rapid loading bunker.

Coalfield (Exposed & Concealed) An area of land above coal measure rocks. A coalfield may be "exposed", i.e. the coal measures are found at the surface, or "concealed" where they are hidden at greater depths beneath younger rocks. Doncaster is situated on a concealed coalfield where the coal measures are buried beneath Magnesian Limestone and Bunter Sandstones.

Drift A sloping tunnel connecting coal seams to the base of the shafts or to the surface.

Fault A geological fracture resulting from the upward or downward movement of rock strata.

Gob The area left following removal of a coal seam. It is supported with waste material or allowed to collapse in a controlled way.

Headgear A structure of wooden, steel lattice or reinforced concrete construction situated above the shafts and used to support the winding wheels.

Heapstead A structure located beneath the headgear providing a covered means of transport for coal exiting the shafts via filled tubs enabling transport to the nearby screens buildings.

Longwall Mining A method of coal working in which coal is mined from a long coal face. The coal face connects two tunnels which lead back to the base of the shafts. The coalface thus advances away from the shafts leaving an area of gob behind. This method was later replaced by retreat mining.

Main A suffix used mainly in South Yorkshire to denote those collieries which mined the largest or main seam from the coal measures, i.e. the Barnsley Seam

Pillar and Stall Mining A method of coal working where coal was extracted from areas known as stalls leaving pillars of coal to support the surface. Largely replaced with longwall mining due to the advance in technology in the 19th Century.

Pit A local term for a coal mine or colliery

Rapid Loading Bunker A large bunker containing many tons of coal which is dropped into railway wagons passing beneath the structure.

Retreat Mining The most economical method in mining in which roadways are driven out to the extremity of the royalty so that a coal face can then be worked back towards the shaft bottom. Largely superseded longwall mining in the 1950s/1960s.

Roadways Underground tunnels leading from the bottom of the shaft to the coal faces.

Royalty An area of land beneath which coal can be extracted by paying a fee or royalty on every ton produced to the landowner.

Screens A building containing numerous devices for sorting individual lumps of coal by size or weight.

Shafts A vertical tunnel from the surface to the coal seam through which the coal is raised and men and materials can access the workings. Following a mining disaster at Hartley Colliery in County Durham each colliery was required to have two shafts, downcast and upcast, to aid escape in the event of an accident. Air was pumped through the downcast shaft to ventilate the workings and then drawn out of the colliery via the upcast shaft.

Shaft Pillar An area of coal left intact in order to support the colliery's surface buildings and thus protect them from the effects of subsidence. Some coal was removed from the shaft pillar to form roadways or tunnels to access the underground workings.

Sinking The process of tunnelling vertically downwards from the surface to the coal seam in order to construct a shaft, usually undertaken by workers called sinkers who specialised in this highly skilled but dangerous work.

Skip Winding A method of winding coal up a shaft by the use of a large capacity metal container or skip. A more economical way of transport than that previously used when individual coal filled tubs were brought to the surface in a cage.

Tubbing A waterproof casing, usually of iron, inserted into a shaft as it was sunk in order to keep back water and soft sediments.

Tubs Small wagons used to transport coal underground, usually hauled by pit ponies.

Washery A surface plant building for dealing with the cleaning and washing of coal

Winding Engine An engine, initially steam driven but later powered by electricity, used to raise the cages up and down the shafts.

Bibliography

Auckland, Clifford (1989). The growth of a township: Maltby's Story. Rotherham MBC Libraries, Museums and Arts Department.

Barnett, A L (1984). The Railways of the South Yorkshire Coalfield from 1880. RCTS Publishing, Devon.

Beastall, T. W. (1975). A North Country Estate, The Lumleys and Saundersons as landowners 1600-1900. Phillimore & Co, London.

Brennan, D. J. & Beckett, Eric (2012). A shaft full of Shadows, Maltby Colliery. Privately Printed.

Colliery Guardian (1927). The Colliery Year Book & Coal Trades Directory. Louis Cassier Publishing, London.

Doncaster Amalgamated Collieries Limited (1944). (A Souvenir Brochure published on the occasion of the visit of the delegation of American Mining Engineers).

Elliott, B. J. (2002). The South Yorkshire Joint Railway & The Coalfield. The Oakwood Press, Monmouthshire.

Elliott, Brian (2009). South Yorkshire Mining Disasters Vol II: The Twentieth Century. Wharncliffe Books, Barnsley.

Finney, Mike (1995). Men of Iron. A History of The Sheepbridge Company. Bannister Publications, Chesterfield.

Hill, Alan (2001). The South Yorkshire Coalfield, a history and development. Tempus Publishing, Stroud.

Kitchen, Fred (1940). Brother to the Ox. J M Dent & Sons, London.

Maltby Coronation Souvenir (1953). Maltby Urban District Council. Maltby.

Maltby Main Colliery (1961) Golden Jubilee 1911-1961. National Coal Board.

Modern Methods of Coal Production and Shipment (no date c1928). Yorkshire Amalgamated Collieries Ltd.

Rodgers, Alice (2008) Souvenir of Maltby Colliery Centenary Celebrations. (Plus unpublished notes)

Tuffrey, Peter (2000). Images of England: Edlington Maltby & Warmsworth. Tempus Publishing Limited, Gloucestershire.

Walters, Sir J Tudor (1927). The Building of Twelve Thousand Houses. Ernest Benn Publishing Ltd, London.

A note on the illustrations

Several of the illustrations are taken from postcards that were published by early photographers who between them produced an incredible body of work recording the transformation of Maltby from rural village to colliery town. These photographers included:

John Crowther-Cox of Rotherham who recorded numerous views of the old village of Maltby in 1906/7 and produced a smashing series of views showing the construction of the SYJR.
Edgar Leonard Scrivens (ELS) who visited Maltby on several occasions, (1908, 1911, 1914, 1925 and 1933) producing over 300 postcards of the township.
Regina Press Photographers of Doncaster who were commissioned by the colliery company to produce a series of views of the colliery and model village in 1910 and 1911.
James Simonton & Sons (JS&S) of Balby who visited Maltby in 1913 and later returned during the interwar period and the early 1950s, capturing the village's transformation during these years.
Doncaster Rotophoto who produced a series of 100 Maltby postcards in 1919, some of which reproduced earlier James Simonton photographs.
Finally, Arjay Productions of Doncaster who visited Maltby in the 1960s capturing a lot of the redevelopment of the High Street area.